I Don't Go to Church

(I Am the Church)

DAVID E. BISH

WestBow Press books may be ordered through booksellers or by contacting:

WestBow Press
A Division of Thomas Nelson & Zondervan
1663 Liberty Drive
Bloomington, IN 47403
www.westbowpress.com
1 (866) 928-1240

ISBN: 978-1-4908-2076-7 (sc)
ISBN: 978-1-4908-2077-4 (hc)
ISBN: 978-1-4908-2075-0 (e)

Library of Congress Control Number: 2013923334

Printed in the United States of America.

WestBow Press rev. date: 12/18/2013

CONTENTS

INTRODUCTION

I've gone to church most of my life. I actually love going to church. You might say—since I'm the founding pastor of a church planted in 1995, with three weekend services, one multisite campus, and a second one in formulation—that I pretty much have to go to church. But the truth of the matter is that I quit going to church a number of years ago. And the reason that I don't go to church anymore is that I discovered that I *am* the church. And if you are a follower of Jesus, so are you. That means you can stop going to church too.

Like many, I spent a great portion of my life with Christ involving myself in the many activities of the church, both as a follower and as a leader. Many of these things were good things, and in spite of my limited understanding, God used them for his purposes. But I began to get disillusioned with people in the church—myself included—when I realized that for all the activity and gatherings, very little was being accomplished with respect to Jesus' mandate to make disciples and love our neighbors. I was frustrated that people were satisfied with simply showing up at a building for a church service on a semiregular schedule, but their hearts for the most part still belonged to their own agendas, and church was just another thing to go to into an already busy schedule of events.

Further, I became even more jaded (not a good thing for a pastor to be) by what seemed to be a growing consumer mindset when it came to the whole idea of going to church. People were going to church for what they could get out of it rather than for what they could contribute to it. This frustration almost led me to a place of despair and wondering if God's hand of blessing was really upon what we were doing in his name. I was so discouraged by the consumers that I was losing sight of the precious people in our church family who really were serving God and loving others. But even as our church was growing numerically, I sensed there was something dysfunctional internally. I decided that we really needed to quit *going* to church.

And God was gracious to give us an idea and some language to help us move out of where we were and into the place he wanted us to be. Not everything we experienced or tried was an entirely new or original idea. I'm sure you'll recognize that as you read this book and elements of our story. These chapters have come out of a series of messages I shared with our church family a few years ago, along with some subsequent seasoning of the concepts and language that have helped us create a culture of *being* the church and not *going* to church. Some of these ideas are theological in nature, as expressed in the character of God and his kingdom. Other elements are more practical and methodological. But when you think about it, both of these elements are necessary in understanding and implementing what the church is really all about.

When our church participated in the pilot REVEAL survey produced by the Willow Creek Association a few years ago, one of the things it showed us was that the culture and language we had created were paying some dividends. We were doing a pretty good job of creating ownership of the mission of Jesus within our church family. Our "I don't go to church; I am the church" philosophy was getting some traction, and since creating ownership was one of the main catalysts for spiritual formation in the REVEAL study's research analysis, we were invited along with a host of other churches to the Willow Creek Association's REVEAL conference to speak about our best practice—namely, why we don't go to church anymore.

Moving our church family closer to owning the mission and ministry for themselves has been one of the greatest rewards—and challenges—of my journey as a spiritual leader. Many have actually resisted this momentum and have gone to other places where they can continue to *go* to church instead of having to wrestle with the idea of actually *being* the church. But for those who, as I say, "get it," a whole new adventure of life transformation and community impact became the reality.

Perhaps you and your church are ready for such a shift. It won't come easy, and many will not understand. Some will, in fact, resist or oppose it. But there's one thing I can guarantee you, and that is that God will have your back on this. He doesn't want you to go to church either. It was never his intention for you to *go* to church. He wants you to *be* the church.

Read on.

CHAPTER 1

THE TALE OF TWO KINGDOMS

> Then the LORD God said, "Look, the human beings have become like us knowing both good and evil. What if they reach out, take fruit from the tree of life, and eat it? Then they will live forever!"
>
> —Genesis 3:22

"Once upon a time . . ." It seems every great story begins that way—even God's, which begins with, well, "In the beginning." And great stories end the same way too—at least they're supposed to. You know, ". . . happily ever after." But what makes the beginnings and endings of such stories so powerful is what happens between "once" and "after." And the same thing is true of God's story—a story that is still being written, by the way. I'd like to suggest that God's story is not just *a* tale of two kingdoms but *the* tale of two kingdoms. Let me show you what I mean. I'll bet you may have already noticed it.

Something happened—somewhere. I mean, really, when you look around at our world and take stock of all the brokenness and waywardness, don't you wonder if life on this planet isn't somehow working out a plan gone terribly wrong? And I'm not just talking about the way the media always plays up all the bad news and scandals; I understand what sells print space and airtime. No, I'm talking about what happens every day in our normal, but arguably messed-up, lives. To quote from one of the lines in the children's book series featuring Madeleine, the cute little French schoolgirl, "Something is not right—something is quite wrong."

And this is true. There is something that is not right—something that is quite wrong. Us. But it wasn't always that way. It wasn't the original plan. What started off as infinitely right and categorically far from wrong was God's plan for humanity. That plan warranted the creation of an incredible and indescribable universe, which of course could only begin to reflect hints of the grandeur and majesty of its maker. This divine creativity then focused on the fabrication of a planet so perfectly situated and so meticulously designed that its final molecular composition would allow for the vibrant inhabitation of the yet-to-be-formed primary object of all this creative genius—that, of course, being people.

All of This for Us

Many have observed and written of this anthropic design template—that is, that God created a finite place within infinite space that would be perfectly suited for human life. It's really incredible when you think about it that God first of all created an ever-expanding universe filled with millions of galaxies playing host to billions of stars. He did that just so he could create one particular galaxy of milky persona, which houses a wonderful (but not particularly extraordinary, compared to some others) star called the sun, which is positioned with such precise tolerances that it neither scorches the human-inhabited sphere nor causes it to become a dark, frozen tomb.

And then, thirdly, in a planetary dance of nine (no, make that eight—I'm still bummed that Pluto got demoted), this beautifully swirled marble of blue and green orbits the energy-rich star with a grace and fluidity that not only marks off days and seasons of time but also receives life and passes it on to the earth's primary residents. God really goes out of his way to get ready for company!

You know how it is when you're expecting company—especially people with whom you're not that well acquainted. The house gets a real going-over. And if you're living in my house with my wonderful wife, four children, and two golden–terrier mix canines, well, there's often some real work to be done. So everything, inside and out, gets some well-deserved attention—far beyond what would have been previously considered acceptable. And for what reason? Guests are coming, and you want things to look great. And you want your guests to feel comfortable. In the same way—but immeasurably more so—God's original work of creation accomplished both of these things.

This world looked great (perfect, in fact) because God created it. And it was made with his guests' comfort in mind. Genesis reminds us of this every time God finishes one element of his creation and offers his own self-evaluation of "and it was good." But it still wasn't great. That doesn't happen until God finally gets to what he's been creating things for all along. After God creates everything else (and I mean everything), he creates people. It's almost like God has hurried through all the preliminary aspects of creation—as formidable as they were—and with unbridled anticipation utters a collective and audible work order: "Let us make man in our image, to be like ourselves" (Genesis 1:26).

Made for So Much More

And while everything he's created up to this point (and again, that's everything) reflects his glory and his majesty, it's this final and ultimate creative work that is designed for not just *reflection* but also *extension.* That's what it means for humanity to be created in the image of God: not to be just a *facsimile* so that the world will see what God is like, but also to be a *prodigy* so that the work and will of God will be active and present in these loyal subjects and in this realm—this newly minted kingdom of God.

And this new kingdom would represent both its creator's glory and his agenda. Or, as Mark Foreman, author of *Wholly Jesus*, writes, "Simply put, the kingdom of God is the ruling domain of God. It is the realm over which he is king and therefore his will is absolute" (p. 82). That's how this newly formed kingdom began. And amazingly, this kingdom of God would invite those created in his image to enjoy a relationship with the King and assist in ruling his kingdom. That was the original plan, at least. But there's the advent of *another* kingdom coming.

Before we get to that—and it doesn't take long in the book of Genesis; it comes in chapter 3, in fact—I want to camp for a while on this idea of God creating us in his image (*Imago Dei*). I've always felt that the way sin shows up so soon is a little disconcerting. Genesis 1–2 records this amazing event of creation, full of divine provision and purpose, only to have everything come unraveled in the third chapter. I mean, just how long did our first parents live in the original product before that fateful day? A week? A couple of months? Certainly not long enough. Anyway, what about their original design and purpose in God's kingdom was *Imago Dei*?

Imago Dei: Kingdom Community

Authors have written entire books on the grand subject of kingdom community, but my purpose here is to make a few simple observations about God's kingdom and the subjects of his kingdom. The first idea is that God created us for the purpose of community—or, more specifically, relationships within community. We get our first clue from the verse quoted earlier. When it came time for the pinnacle of his creation, God said, "Let us make man in our image." Did you notice he said "us" and "our?" He uses the second person plural forms of the pronoun. God is, himself, community. Though the word "trinity" is not found anywhere in Scripture, God has revealed himself as such (God the Father, God the Son, and God the Holy Spirit) through the implications of many passages throughout the Bible. This one in Genesis is the first; and it is perhaps the most significant, because it occurs in the context of his creative will and purpose. Therefore, to be created in the image of God is to be created in and for community.

Imago Dei: Kingdom Completion

Another aspect of our nature, which is closely related to the idea of community, is found in Genesis 2:18: "Then the LORD God said, 'It is not good for the man to be alone. I will make a helper who is just right for him.'" Evidently, by creating only the man, God's work was only partially in his image. In fact, the word translated as "helper" in this verse would be better understood as "completer." In other words, the man was not yet in the image of God because he was still incomplete. There's a divine wholeness in God's triune nature of Father, Son, and Spirit. The absence of any one of them would render God incomplete. I've also noticed in Genesis 2 that God may have been trying to awaken Adam to this reality by giving him an interesting and, I have to conclude, exhaustive task. Right after God says he's going to make a "helper" for the first man, and just before he puts him to sleep to do so, he has Adam give names to all the animals. It was probably fun at first, but I would think that the challenge to come up with names at all—let alone creative ones for every amazing specimen—was pretty daunting by the end of the project.

I also think Adam began to get distracted at some point in the process too. Think about it. All these birds and animals filed by under the divine leadership of their creator so that Adam could participate with God in this work of creation. This scene, illustrating how humanity rules with God, provides another clue to an alternative meaning of Imago Dei that we'll get to later. And so they pass by . . . Mr. and Mrs. Giraffe . . . Mr. and Mrs. Hippopotamus . . . Mr. and Mrs. Rhinoceros . . . (Pretty creative names so far, don't you think?). And so it goes—all these marvelous animals, and their mates! And Adam no doubt began to put this all together in his head. He must have been thinking to himself, *All these boy animals have girlfriends. What about mine?* The text even alludes to this when it states, "He gave names to all the livestock, all the birds of the sky, and all the wild animals. But there was still no helper just right for him" (Genesis 2:20). Still there was no helper just right for him. But not for long.

As the mostly familiar story goes, God placed the man under a firm anesthetic and formed a woman from a rib taken from the man. In the Hebrew, the suffix "from" is added to the word "man" to make the word for "woman." She was made "from" the man and "for" the man. This doesn't mean she is less than the man, however. On the contrary, it's not until her arrival on the scene that the man is complete—the way God always intended for him to be. The record is clear in this verse: "So God created human beings [literal, "man"] in his own image. In the image of God he created them; male and female he created them" (Genesis 1:27). And so God remedied Adam's incompleteness and what he lacked in being created in the image of God by creating a woman (the name Adam gave her) not just to be his companion but also to make him complete.

When God said that it wasn't good for the man to be alone, he wasn't talking about loneliness. He was talking about finishing what it meant to create man in the image of God. Eve wasn't created so Adam wouldn't be lonely; she was created so that they would reflect the essence of God in community. And this relational community would have both masculine and feminine characteristics—just as God does. And in the context of this diverse community, there would be love. This was the very first marriage—and love in a marriage is supposed to reveal something about God himself!

Let me say here, as an aside, that love in the community context is not just limited to husbands and wives, as there are many in the story that God is still writing who find themselves in sorrowful places of isolation or broken relationships. But the kingdom of God is broader than just the context of marriage, as wonderful and as God-ordained as that is. We'll see in the chapters to follow that God's kingdom is designed for all those who love him—that they may find their place and experience their rightful and intended belonging to God and one another. Those dispossessed throughout the Old Testament would find their hope and refuge in God's bigger family—and that's the exact DNA that would characterize the early church as well. Those without spouses would be cared for. Those without parents would be mothered and fathered by fellow believers. Those without families would have a prolific number of brothers and sisters. Those who were forgotten would be noticed. And those who were ostracized would be welcomed. And, I might add, it looked a lot like love.

Imago Dei: Kingdom Love

That brings me to a third observation. God's original kingdom was not just a community (a king and his subjects) and holistically complete, but an unbroken community of love. In addition to being created for community and wholeness, man was also created to love and be loved—something that can never exist outside of community or completeness. Now love is an even more exhaustive topic than the two we've already covered, so let me just make a couple of points here, with plans to unpack it further in a later chapter. The love that exists between human beings is supposed to be of the brand and nature of the love God has for us—specifically, it is to be unconditional, sacrificial, and without any expectation of a return. That's why Paul's inspired words in the fifth chapter of Ephesians characterize the love a man has for his wife as being like the love Christ has for his church (also referred to as the bride of Christ). This depth of love, however, was to be extended to all others, not just a spouse. Jesus would extend loving others to the very perimeter of even loving our enemies.

And so, with the same motivation for loving as that found in God, the nature of this deep and sincere loving is *voluntary*. It is also *covenantal*. It is voluntary because God has given man the ability to think and make choices about how to act or respond. Though I won't expound on it here, choice is another byproduct of being created in the image of God. Love, by its very nature, is always a choice. And the choice is not contingent on how the other person loves or responds to love. That's the idea of a covenant. It's a promise. It's a vow. It chooses to love the other person unconditionally and selflessly, whether or not that person deserves it or reciprocates it. That's why God doesn't have a contract with man, but rather a covenant. A covenant is characterized by grace (undeserved love and favor), while a contract speaks of something one is owed or has earned. God keeps his promise to us no matter what. He invites us to love him in return out of our own free will. He doesn't refuse to love us if we don't love him back, and he'll never force us to love him. (I'm not even sure he can; that's the nature of love—willing and unforced.) And if God loves us this way, and we are created in his image, then we are to love this way too.

Imago Dei: Kingdom Royalty

Consequently, the kingdom of God would reflect the nature and character of God, its King, in this primary attribute of God—a community of unconditional love. And that's exactly what the kingdom of God looked like in the beginning. There was community. There was completeness. There was love. And there was something else: reigning. Not only did he create us to be like him with respect to living in complete community with selfless loving as the chief operational policy, but he also invited his human prodigy into the care and management of his kingdom. In other words, he invited mankind to help him *rule* over it. This is what seems obvious when "God blessed them and said, 'Be fruitful and multiply. Fill the earth and govern it. Reign over the fish in the sea, the birds in the sky, and all the animals that scurry along the ground . . .' then God looked over all that he had made, and he saw that it was very good" (Genesis 1:28, 31). Do you see that? Now God says it was *very* good.

I love what the Hebrew language does here. Because there is no word for the adverb "very," the Hebrew emphatic simply repeats the adjective. So in the case of "very good," the literal translation would be "good, good." Up until this moment, everything God has created (everything except man, that is) has been good. Now don't get me wrong; good, when God makes it, is better than any other kind of good. But now it's "good, good." In other words, it's finished, or better, or complete—great!

Imago Dei: Kingdom Harmony

And as we have said, it's in the being complete, or very good, that creation can go on reflecting the image of God and fulfilling the purposes of God. The Hebrews had a word to describe such "completeness" and purposeful harmony—it's the word "shalom." We normally see this word translated as "peace," and that's not incorrect. But the idea goes beyond just the absence of conflict (which is how we often regard the idea of peace) to include the idea that things are the way they're supposed to be and consequently everything is working as it should. And the byproduct of such harmonious function is always shalom. Shalom is what God's kingdom was like before things changed. Everything was just right, everything was functioning as it had been designed to function, everything was integrated perfectly, and there was an overwhelming existential reality of peace.

Everything was right with the world. Man was in harmony with God and each other the way the Father, Son, and Holy Spirit were within the Trinity. There was perfect, selfless, unconditional love between all parties, much like the three notes of a triad chord in music. Played separately, they sound just fine; played together, they sound more like music. And God invites us to the song. Man being made in God's image was not only a part of God's created kingdom; we were assisting in it as well. We would collaborate with God in procreating and managing and ruling his ongoing creation.

Imago Dei: Kingdom Creativity

This leads us to a final observation related to being made in the image of God—we were created to *create*! We are not just creation. We are also creative. Bearing the image of God in the context of his kingdom means that we share in the blessing of what it means to receive from him, as well as the blessings of ruling, creating, and sharing with others. We are, in fact, an extension of God's creativity, and when that creativity is channeled toward the good things and good plans of God, it reflects his character and fulfills his agenda.

Through our creative design we perpetuate the life God began in our first parents by enabling them to create humans of their own, children. They extend the pattern for loving communities called families, where God is included, and this love provides for our basic human need to belong. And as mentioned previously, in cases where marriage and children may not be our station in life, God's larger family fulfills his plan for including everyone in his kingdom.

Also, our individual and unique God-given aptitudes bring variety and fullness to our roles within God's kingdom. No one can be all-creative on his or her own, but we can all be all-creative together. It's the perpetual creativity and energy for blessing that God has instilled in every man and woman that also marked the nature of his original kingdom. Everyone was loving the other and working in harmony for the principles and purposes of God and his kingdom. It made God extremely proud to observe his children succeeding, and he loved providing for their every need. It was paradise.

Another Kingdom

But this perfect kingdom was about to experience a cosmic trauma that would usher in another kingdom—a weak and destructive counterpart to the King's original design. This was always a possibility, given the constructs of free will and man's ability to make choices. And the Creator King planned it that way. And regarding what happened next, let's just say he wasn't surprised.

As I mentioned earlier, it's amazing that this comprehensive cosmic shift happens in the third chapter of Genesis. Would it have been such a big deal to make it to chapter six? Yeah, six, the biblically significant "number of man," seems to be a more appropriate chapter for such a thing. But then again, the chapter and verse thing came later, so who knows. And when I really ponder my own propensities for straying and being distracted, chapter three doesn't sound so unrealistic after all. So the story launches with the marvelous creation account in Genesis chapters one and two—and then, like a dark cloud, chapter three. Enter, another kingdom.

This *other* kingdom is not God's original design or intent, but it is the consequence of choosing another king over the rightful one. The chances that things will change (for good or for not-so-good) when a new ruler takes the throne are almost universally predictable. We have all experienced such angst during presidential campaigns. Regardless of what side you're on—or whether your candidate is in or out—our elation or lack thereof is primarily based on whether our preferred agenda is in play. The king who best reflects what I want in a kingdom is the king I want on the throne, even if I have to make a few concessions to have the best possible option. And if it were a possibility, what could be a better choice for a new king than . . . well, me?

King Me

This is why the Bible says that the Serpent was the shrewdest or craftiest of all the animals God had created. This Devil-incarnate creature knew better than to suggest himself as the best possible candidate for the new post, although that's what his prideful, evil disposition craved. And since he wasn't able to oust God from his rightful throne by himself, he would catalyze a coup d'état that would advertise self-rule as the new rule. And his plan would work—not if he lured our first parents to vote for him, but if he simply persuaded them *not* to vote for God. And so his devious campaign speech was embraced in proverbial hook, line, and sinker fashion. Genesis chapter three records their consequentially destructive choice and the evolution of their demise.

And ever since that choice was made, mankind has been captivated by this self-imposed independence and authority known as sin. Sin is merely the willful decision to live according to your own agenda rather than God's. It's a matter of doing your will as opposed to God's will. The cleverness of the Evil One to use our own pride against us was masterfully deceptive and effective. And so we're all born into this world with the desire to be king, to run our own life, and to chart our own course. "King Me" has a nice ring to it. And after all, who knows better how to take care of me than me? I'd answer that question with another question, made popular by TV psychologist Dr. Phil: "How's that working for you?"

What Did God Really Say?

Speaking of probing questions, here is the one the Enemy used to deceive our first parents—and it all begins with doubt: "Did God really say you must not eat the fruit of any of the trees in the garden?" (Genesis 3:1). The woman replies with the prerehearsed prescription for fruit-gathering, citing that only the tree in the middle of the garden is off limits. But there's a hint of doubt in the question itself, as if the Devil is raising the issue of whether they even heard God correctly in the first place. And even if they heard him rightly, maybe their interpretation is skewed. Then—and I get the impression Satan jumps in even before Eve finishes her previous statement—he interrupts her with the bold and authoritative statement "You won't die! God knows that your eyes will be opened as soon as you eat it, and you will be like God, knowing both good and evil" (Genesis 3:4). So on the heels of doubt comes contradiction. Doubt casts a shadow of uncertainty on the mandate, and then the contradiction poses the possibility that God is holding something back from his subjects when it comes to co-reigning in his kingdom. And if that wasn't enough, doggone it, "the tree was beautiful and its fruit looked delicious, and she wanted the wisdom it would give her" (Genesis 3:6). It just looked too good to pass up. She was convinced, the Bible says, and apparently so was her husband (who was there too, by the way), and they ate. Never had a meal choice cost so much.

In my humanness, I've often wondered what the big deal was about eating a piece of fruit. And I feel bad for the apple, because it's taken the historical blame for what the text refers to only as fruit. Maybe the mango has gotten off free all this time! But you must realize that this is not just about forbidden fruit; it's about independence and impeachment. Our first parents' choice—a universal and far-reaching one at that—was ultimately about this idea of kingship and rule. They decided to remove the rightful king (in whose image they had been made and with whom they had been invited to rule) and place themselves on the throne. What they couldn't have anticipated, however, is that in doing so they weren't going to be kings ruling over this original existing kingdom, but that they would inaugurate an entirely new and different kingdom over which their reign would exist. Thus, the tale of two kingdoms.

Kingdoms in Conflict

Interestingly, you might think that once the subsequent kingdom took root, the original kingdom would disappear or be abdicated. Not so. The kingdoms actually coexist. Jesus referred to this in particular in his parable of the wheat and the weeds:

Here is another story Jesus told:

> The Kingdom of Heaven is like a farmer who planted good seed in his field. But that night as the workers slept, his enemy came and planted weeds among the wheat, then slipped away. When the crop began to grow and produce grain, the weeds also grew.
>
> The farmer's workers went to him and said, "Sir, the field where you planted that good seed is full of weeds! Where did they come from?"
>
> "An enemy has done this!" the farmer exclaimed.
>
> "Should we pull out the weeds?" they asked.

> "No," he replied, "you'll uproot the wheat if you do. Let both grow together until the harvest. Then I will tell the harvesters to sort out the weeds, tie them into bundles, and burn them, and to put the wheat in the barn." (Matthew 13:24–30)

This, too, is a part of God's plan. It's not as though the fall of man (the choice that commenced sin in the world) caught God off guard or came as a surprise. He knew it would happen. He didn't *cause* it to happen, but he *knew* it would happen, and he allowed it to happen. And he also has allowed, from that very first moment on, for his kingdom to operate simultaneously with this other kingdom—what the Scripture refers to elsewhere as the kingdom of this world. Make no mistake; both of these polar-opposite kingdoms are real, and they are both spiritual, and they are both present even now as I write this sentence. And as is always the case with kingdoms, they are reflective of their kings—be that a good thing or not.

Good and Evil

Speaking of good (and evil) there's a very important idea regarding sin and its relative choices in a person's life. I used to think that God's admonition to Adam and Eve seemed confusing. They were not permitted to eat from the Tree of the Knowledge of Good and Evil—on the pain of death, no less. But isn't that the point in knowing and following God—that is, knowing the difference between good and evil and choosing the former? And what exactly did he mean by "die" if in fact they didn't really die until hundreds of years after opting for another kingdom? In more recent days I think I've gained some clarity to this issue.

First, the good and evil thing. I don't struggle so much with the existence of evil as I see it as the absence of good—rather than a created entity of its own. For if it were created, then God (who is the Creator of all things) would somehow be responsible for it. But as the absence of good, it is the consequence for substituting an inferior definition for good in the place of the right and original one. That's essentially what happened when our first parents made their dubious choice. You see, they weren't making the choice to eat the fruit for the purpose of understanding the *difference* between good and evil as much as they were making the choice to begin *determining* for themselves what good and evil would be. There's a profound distinction between *knowing* what's good and evil and *establishing* what's good and evil. In other words, mankind (the new king) decides the new boundaries and the new rules, the new morality, and the new right and new wrong. And if there was ever a case where newer isn't better, it's this one.

Another idea that goes along with this dilemma goes back to the fact that being created in God's image is about being able to make choices in the first place. I've come to this conclusion: For there to be a *choice* between good and evil, there had to be a *choice* between good and evil. Or, put another way, the choice to excise God from our life is a choice to remove good, because evil is the absence of good. There are no other alternatives to removing the rightful (good) King and assuming the throne for ourselves. And so, like Eve and Adam, we become convinced that we know better, or that we at least know best how to live our lives. And that means we must determine for ourselves what is right and what is wrong. And in doing so, we no longer bear the image of the Creator King.

Surely, You Shall Die

That's where death comes in. When Adam and Eve chose to be their own king, they lost their co-reign with God. When they decided to be their own gauge of goodness, they lost their innocence. When they decided to live independent of a relationship in community with God, their own relationships suffered. And when they decided to live their own lives without God, they lost what gave them real life in the first place—the Spirit, or the internal presence of God. After all, man was a lifeless lump of clay until God breathed his own breath (Spirit) into him. "Air" and "spirit" are both translated from the same original word. It wasn't just air that filled Adam with life; it was God.

To choose a life with God is real life. To choose a life without God is death. And God let them make those choices. He didn't go running after them to try to cut a deal. If they wanted to call the shots, he would let them. And if only good choices exist in the original kingdom being ruled by the only Good King, then what we have left is a tainted, perverted, cheap imitation of what our destiny was supposed to be. And in doing so we forfeit the community, completeness, love, royalty, harmony, and creativity we were made for. The choice was a possibility all along. And then the choice became a reality. And now there are two kingdoms instead of just one. And it's been that way for a long time.

CHAPTER 2

THE RESURGENCE OF GOD'S KINGDOM

> In those days John the Baptist came to the Judean wilderness and began preaching. His message was, 'Repent of your sins and turn to God, for the Kingdom of Heaven is near.'
>
> —Matthew 3:1–2

In his book *Tipping Point*, author Malcolm Gladwell makes the case for the phenomenon that his title describes. He proposes that the pandemic growth of certain widespread movements have, at some earlier point, been sparked by an event or catalyst. In one example he recounts the recent rise in popularity among celebrities (and subsequently the rest of humanity) with the Hush Puppies brand of shoes. You may remember those comfy, suede upper / foam lower casual-wear loafers. I think I may have had a pair once, come to think of it. They really were comfortable. A little plain, but comfortable.

In any case, what started as a few street kids in the Bronx sporting these leather throwbacks has catapulted into a shoe fashion tsunami. Sales rocketed, and when the research explaining this curious boom in sales was traced back to celebrity-pirated street fashion, everyone was amazed—amazed at what tipped the scales. Thus, the tipping point.

Remember those two kingdoms from chapter one? They've been coexisting from that fateful day when man opted to rule for himself. God's kingdom did not vanish and was not abdicated; it just became less visible, to put it mildly. The kingdom of *self*, however, gained a lot of momentum, and the evidence of this godless and rebellious enterprise has a long history—and a current head of steam. But the less obvious kingdom of God would mount a comeback—and there's a tipping-point story of the spiritual brand found here too.

One of the most important storylines that the Bible chronicles is the way God's kingdom and his relentless love for his wayward children is at work, gaining a momentum of its own. This is detailed first in the Old Testament as God reenters the atmosphere of humanity via the people of Israel, and then in the New Testament in the advent of Jesus Christ and the birth of this beautiful thing called the church. And Jesus' arrival on the scene is unquestionably the tipping point of this story. And for me it has been this better, clearer understanding of God's revealed kingdom and the true nature of the church that led me to a recent decision. I'm never *going* to church again.

Church in the Old Days

Now, before you write me off and close this book, I assure you that in the next chapter, I'm going to explain in more detail what I mean when I say *I don't go to church.* I suspect even the subtitle has given you some indication of where I'm heading. But first, I want to trace in a somewhat abbreviated fashion the record of the unveiling of God's kingdom prior to the church age. Brace yourself. We're going to cover a lot of ground in a short number of pages.

It is impossible to fathom the depth of loss our first parents felt when the reality of their decision to rule their own lives set in. I picture them in my mind as walking out and away from the paradise that had been their harmonious home—not holding hands this time, as they would normally have done during their cool evening strolls in the garden with God. Numb now from God's painful declaration of their eviction and the subsequent curses and consequences of their self-ruled life, they must have remained silent for a time with momentary glances back at a garden entrance now blocked by angelic sentries. But in their countenance you could clearly read their thoughts: *My God, what have we done?*

In their journey away from the garden (and from God), they mentally recounted all the things they were losing. There would be no more enjoyment of God's wonderful provisions; there would be sweat and toil for mere survival. There would be no more joy in working and managing God's possessions; there would be striving and scraping, and the unfulfilled desire for more. There would still be the extension of life through childbirth, but evidently pain would now be associated with that process. Ladies, doesn't it make you wonder what having children would have been like in a world with no sin? Wow!

And so they calculated their losses, scenario after painful scenario. And then I imagine their silence may have been broken as they looked into each other's tear-stained faces and asked, "Wanna know what I miss most of all?" And then, in audible unison, they would reply, "Being with our Father."

It was truly their greatest loss. And along with it, their once-reflected image of God would be tarnished and flawed. There would be traces and glimpses of the life that had left them—like the shiny paint on the inside of an old, weathered car's door—an unfortunate reminder of a beauty that once was. That same hidden beauty is still there in all of us. And God would begin a timetable for drawing it out in full measure. It began with a guy named Abram.

A Reunion of Sorts

Genesis, chapters 4 through 11, records the increasing fallout of this new kingdom's agenda. Man becomes increasingly (and, for God's part, intolerably) wicked—so much so that God regrets that he ever created him in the first place. And in a couple of extraordinary events (namely, the great flood and the building of the Tower of Babel—Genesis 6–11), God destroys humanity in large part and scatters abroad those who would come after Noah, still not having learned the lesson. And for a time, God leaves the building—not entirely, but there is very little evidence of his original kingdom, and his interaction with man is mostly vindictive and isolated. Yet God is growing homesick for his children.

Enter Abram. Or, I guess I should say, enter God to Abram. It's important to note that Abram wasn't out looking for God. God came calling on Abram. Now, Abram was a pagan living life in a harsh world like everyone else. But there was something God liked about him. It wasn't that he was an especially good man; he was just a man. It wasn't that he had earned God's favor in any way; he had done nothing of the sort. But God knew something about Abram that Abram probably didn't even know himself—he was simply waiting for an opportunity to *believe*.

For God, this was his way of tapping humanity on the shoulder and saying, "Excuse me, I know it's been a while, but I'd really love it if we could get back together again. I really miss being with you, and I've got a plan for making things right again." And there seem to be two important things going on here: (1) God initiates, and (2) Abram responds. It would become the matrix for a few thousand years of interaction between God and mankind. God initiates. Man responds. Even the early church leader John recognized where love originates when he wrote, "We love him because he loved us first" (1 John 4:19).

Believing and Blessing

And so Abram does respond. For God, responding is believing. Notice there are also two aspects to this believing: (1) a leaving and (2) a blessing. The first thing God says to Abram is, "Leave your native country, your relatives, and your father's family, and go to the land that I will show you. I will make you into a great nation. I will bless you and make you famous, and you will be a blessing to others" (Genesis 12:1–2). I can't help but recognize an amazing contrast between our first parents' lonely walk away from God's real estate and Abram's invitation to come back to it. It's a beautiful picture of grace and restoration. In essence, God is inviting Abram back to his roots, his real home, and his rightful place as a divine-inheriting, image-bearing child. He's instructed to leave *his* country and *his* relatives and *his* father's family—in other words, the family and kingdom of *man*. God was inviting him back to the original kingdom, and with that always comes blessing.

So Abram responds with unquestioned leaving. And don't you find it amazing that he packs up and goes without even knowing the final destination? It's as though Abram says to God, "*So, where are we going?*" and God says, "*I'll tell you when we get there.*" The writer of the New Testament book of Hebrews recollects it this way: "It was by faith that Abraham obeyed God when he called him to leave home and go to another land that God would give him as his inheritance. He went without knowing where he was going" (Hebrews 11:8).

God gives this unwavering obedience a name: *faith*. And with it comes a new name for Abram: *Abraham*. His new name is indicative of a new relationship—a restored relationship with God. His new name is indicative of his adoption into his new family—the family of God. His new names naturalizes him into his new country—the kingdom of God. And this invitation would come to include more than just the family of this shepherd from Ur of the Chaldees.

The blessing, of course, is a restored relationship with the Creator and God of the original (and up until now) unrecognized kingdom. And the blessing would get passed on to others as well. Remember the words in Genesis 12: "I will bless you and make you famous and you will be a blessing to others." I believe the blessing is threefold: (1) Being a part of God's family again, Abram and his entourage would enjoy the promise of God's provision, just as had been the case during the good old days in the garden. (2) Being restored to a relationship with God, Abram and company would experience divine community again—just as had been the case when Adam and Eve fellowshipped with him in the cool of the day. (3) The blessing of knowing the one true God would be passed on to others, multiplying the size and breadth of God's restored family. The kingdom would become visible again, and others who would observe it and benefit from the blessings of this newly formed family would themselves be invited to the reunion. And the invitation wasn't just for Abraham's people, but also for all the nations. God chose a particular man and subsequently a race of people to be reconnected to God, but they were also to be his emissaries, showing the rest of the world that God was back in the house and was offering terms of peace. Much later, the prophet Isaiah would record this intention: "Don't let foreigners who commit themselves to the LORD say, 'The LORD will never let me be a part of his people.' And don't let the eunuchs say, 'I'm a dried-up tree with no children and no future . . . I will also bless the foreigners who commit themselves to the Lord, who serve him and love his name''' (Isaiah 56:3, 6a).

Blessing and Promise

Finally, with the invitation came a promise. Often the word "covenant" is used. The Abrahamic covenant was the first of a succession of God's relational commitments to stand by his children and love them no matter what. He would keep his covenant promise in spite of their regular and often wholesale rebellion. Why? Because a covenant isn't conditional. A covenant is a promise to love and be faithful regardless of what the other party does. And that's the way God loves his children.

Throughout the Old Testament, we read about the rollercoaster ride God has with his people. But God is in this for the long haul. He is the God of Abraham, Isaac, and Jacob; and Moses, Joshua, and David, from whose line would eventually come the ultimate offspring of God's homecoming—Jesus, the Son. Though a shaky one, God's relationship with his Imago Dei children would continue through the golden days of Israel and onto the prophets and their ongoing pleas on God's behalf for Israel to not revert to the other kingdom. But they would continually do so. And then, after a four-hundred-year intertestamental sigh of silence, the original kingdom will become more visible. The tipping point is near.

Jesus and his Church

Not since Adam, before the fall of man, had there been a walking, talking human example of God's original intent. That would change in the supernatural birth of his Son, Jesus. God knew all along that simply inviting people back into his kingdom through faith would be difficult for sinful humanity to grasp, so he would have to show them an example of what that would really look like. What would it look like if a human being were to really live up to the practical outworking of the original design? It would look like someone who had manifested the wholeness of body, mind, and spirit in such a way that the true character of God would be revealed. It would look like consistent and unconditional love for those with a willingness to care more about the welfare of others than their own. It would look like the harmonious community, completeness, and humility represented in the Trinitarian Godhead. It would look like Jesus.

And if I'm discerning this correctly, I think I can hear in God's voice the love and pleasure he once felt for our first parents when he sincerely and audibly utters these words at Jesus' baptism: "As Jesus came up out of the water, he saw the heavens splitting apart and the Holy Spirit descending on him like a dove. And a voice from heaven said, 'You are my dearly loved Son, and you bring me great joy'" (Mark 1:10, 11). I believe God missed being able to say that about all of us. And now, through Jesus, he's able to say it again!

But Jesus came for more than just *reflecting* God's original kingdom; he came to *establish* it. And he would do that by paying the price for original sin and offering new life in the Spirit. Once again, the harmony and completeness of the Trinity presented in the creation itself would take part in this promise-fulfilling, re-creation. And out of this fulfillment would arise a new entity that represented God's restored relationship with man and the visible reengagement of his kingdom. I am speaking, of course, of the church. Let's look first at forgiveness.

You Are Forgiven

Most of us who grew up in the church heard a lot about the need for God's forgiveness, and that Jesus' dying on the cross made that possible. There is no truth more wonderful than this. When sin and self-rule separated our first parents from their communion with God, it was also translated forward to everyone who would ever be born into humanity—or of the flesh, as the Bible refers to it. This is why it is crucial that Jesus wasn't born "of the flesh." As the Scripture records in both Old Testament prophecy and New Testament history, Jesus' mother Mary was a virgin and was chosen by God to conceive the Holy Spirit. Her child would be fully human and fully divine.

The reason that this is so crucial to our restoration to God is that for Jesus to die for the sin of humanity, he had to be human and capable of death. And for Jesus to be an acceptable sacrifice for the sin of humanity, he would have to live a perfect life—fulfilling the full letter of God's law—and reflect in his human existence the precise image of God. And to do that he would have to be God. Or, as Paul puts it in 2 Corinthians 5:21, "For God made Christ, who never sinned, to be the offering for our sin, so that we could be made right with God through Christ." Therefore, what Adam accomplishes in one act of willful disobedience (bringing sin to humanity), Jesus reverses in one act of submissive obedience (sin being taken away).

So for the believer, the cross represents a payment for our sin that is complete and effective—or, as the book of Hebrews (chapter 10) describes it, ". . . once and for all." As far as forgiveness is concerned, it's a done deal. Jesus paid it all. It is finished. There's no more that can be done regarding the remedy of our sin—and there's no more that needs to be done. *You are forgiven.* Once in a while I'll be having a discussion with someone about this issue, and the person will say, "Oh, I don't think God can forgive me. I've done a lot of really bad stuff"; to which I always delight in replying, "It's too late! He already has—in Christ!" But hear me when I say that Jesus didn't just come to die on the cross to take away our sin, despite how wonderful and necessary as that is. He also came to give us life.

You Need New Life

You see, the cross and forgiveness are only one side of the salvation coin. Like any coin, it has two sides. And if the one side of the coin of salvation is forgiveness, then the other side of the coin is life—life in the Spirit. Remember that I said in the first chapter that Adam *wasn't* given life because God breathed air into him; he had life because God place his Spirit (Greek, *pneuma)* into him. Coming back to God's original kingdom and being adopted into God's spiritual family requires this new life—or, as the gospel writer John likes to put it, being "born again." That's why the resurrection is so vital to this whole mission. We didn't just need someone to pay our debt. We needed someone to bring us back to life—the spiritual life our first parents had before they lost it.

What I'm saying is that Jesus died on the cross for *all* the sin of *all* the world. But that doesn't mean that everyone has experienced salvation. It's not until a person believes in Jesus and puts his or her faith in this finished work of forgiveness and surrenders his or her life back to God that the miracle of new life is bestowed. In essence, it's just like reversing the decision our first parents made when they took God off the throne of their lives and inaugurated a totally new kingdom of their own. Now, with the price of their disobedience (and ours too) paid for, we are free to step down off the throne of our lives and defect from this inferior kingdom, putting God back on the throne—where he rightfully belongs.

Life in the Spirit

So now the stage is set. Jesus becomes a man to bring forgiveness to mankind. Jesus rises from the dead to ensure the acceptance of his sacrifice and claim victory over sin and death. Just one more detail remains: Pentecost. Pentecost was a Jewish celebration, and it would be on this day that God would inaugurate a strategic revelation of his kingdom. Another tipping point, if you will. Jesus had spent three years with his disciples, teaching them and showing them what life in the original kingdom was supposed to look like. And after his death and resurrection, he warned them not to do anything or go anywhere until the Holy Spirit arrived. The day that this happened is the day we refer to as the birth of the church. And so they heeded his warning and waited together until what is recorded in Acts chapter 2 took place: "All the believers were meeting together in one place. Suddenly, there was a sound from heaven like a mighty windstorm, and it filled the house where they were sitting. Then, what looked like flames of fire or tongues of fire appeared and settled on each of them. And everyone present was filled with the Holy Spirit and began speaking in other languages, as the Holy Spirit gave them this ability" (Acts 2:1–4).

And though they are not specifically referred to as the church as yet, it is the completed mission of Jesus' earthly life and the subsequent commissioning of his disciples to fulfill the purposes of God's kingdom, that bring their new reality into being. In fact, in a later chapter we'll take a closer look at Jesus' teaching on the "kingdom of God," which is how he always described a return to this original and better way of life.

I was nine years old when I surrendered my life back to God's rule—at least as much as a nine-year-old is able to appropriate. But my understanding of what it meant to follow Christ would crystallize over the years. Through various experiences and divine superintending, I would realize that what God originally intended for Adam—and what was fully actualized in the life of Jesus Christ—would begin to form my own understanding of life in God's resurgent kingdom.

So What Exactly Is the Church?

So are you still wondering why I don't go to church? I know I'm taking my good old time getting to the answer to that, but I don't want to assume that everyone reading this book understands how our perception of what the church is got so messed up in the first place, and how we can correct that. I hope you've been grasping so far that we've been talking about God and his *kingdom*—the Old Testament version, where it was progressively being reintroduced—and about how the New Testament tipping point, with the advent of the person and work of Jesus Christ, has drawn it very near. The church, then, is essentially the visible presence of God in the world as his kingdom draws closer to its final and complete restoration. As theologians have suggested, it is in some ways *already* and in other ways *not yet.*

So we must begin seeing (if we don't already) that the church is God's kingdom. God's kingdom was primarily seated and heralded in the people of Israel in the Old Testament, and it experiences a transition into what we know as the church in the New Testament. God's kingdom via the church continues to the present. This church of Jesus Christ cannot be confined to organizations, institutions, denominations, doctrinal distinctions or places of worship. All of these and many other descriptors have been mistakenly embraced as the church, but they are not just inadequate; they are also incorrect.

These erroneous misconceptions have been marinating for decades, if not centuries. The same errors that led the Jewish people to misinterpret the law's purpose, leading them to create a system of false religion, are still present. The selfishness and false piety that confronted Jesus and his reinterpretations of the kingdom of heaven are alive and well in many Christian arenas today. It manifests itself in legalism, spiritual arrogance, cultures of exclusiveness, irrelevance, and, perhaps most detrimental of all, a wholesale lack of love.

It's this very impression that religion gives of Christians—and of Christ—that has been the major catalyst for many people not going to church anymore, or not going to church at all. And honestly, I don't blame them. But unfortunately what they're rejecting isn't what Jesus or the church are really all about. Actually, I don't *go* to church for some of the same reasons.

I guess it's time I told you why.

CHAPTER 3

WHY YOU SHOULDN'T GO TO CHURCH

> Now he is far above any ruler or authority or power or leader or anything else—not only in this world but also in the world to come. God has put all things under the authority of Christ and has made him head over all things for the benefit of the church.
>
> And the *church* is his body; it is made full and complete by Christ, who fills all things everywhere with himself.
>
> —Ephesians 1:21–23, emphasis mine

I can't remember not going to church. My family and I were churchgoers from my early childhood. The memories I have are favorable. The church I attended wasn't perfect, but it wasn't horrible either. I'd also have to say that, over the years, we were pretty regular attenders. That's what good Christians did on Sunday morning—*go* to church. Really good Christians went to church on Sunday evening as well. And if you went back on Wednesday night, well, let's just say the only place you could go from there was heaven.

God did some really wonderful things in my life in those early days of going to church, though it wasn't at church that I surrendered my life to Christ. It was actually a vacuum cleaner salesman visiting our home who led my father to Jesus. I like to say he helped clean up our act. In the years that followed, Sunday school and youth group were formative in my spiritual journey. Later, in college (a secular one), my more sheltered life was peeled back and my faith benefited from what I call "life in the real world." Thankfully, that experience propelled my relationship with Christ instead of dismantling it, and I experienced for the first time what I can only describe as authentic biblical community. Other Christ-following peers helped me understand the need for others in my relationship with God and assisted me in seeing more clearly my role and responsibility in his kingdom. "Kingdom" you say? And some lights begin to go on.

I probably need to say at this point that I grew more spiritually in my first six months of college than I had in the previous nine years since my conversion. I'd have to say the main reasons for this were having to own my faith more independently and the discipleship-oriented community of other, more seasoned followers of Christ. It also dawned on me that this holistic life in Christ had very little to do with where we met or on what day (our group met on Tuesday nights), but more to do with our being a community of believers who incorporated our devotion to Jesus in all areas of our lives. Of course we attended a local church and I developed a great relationship with the pastor—but I was becoming a 24-7-365 follower of Jesus, and it wasn't really connected to going to church.

After those defining years of growth and perspective in college, I went on to teach in a public school for four years, met and married Lori (the love of my life since June 15, 1985), graduated from a seminary in the Midwest, experienced the blessing of four children (all young adults now), served as a youth pastor for five years, and then, in 1995, planted the church where I currently serve as the lead pastor. The last seventeen plus years have been an incredible journey, and many of the views I express in this book have been incubated in that context. I am so grateful to God for the people and ministry of Tri-County Church.

I know that's a really fast rundown of my history, but I wanted to give you a little more personal information on my background. You see, I'm not at all against going to church as it relates to the weekend services millions of people attend each week all over the world. As the primary teaching pastor in our fellowship, I go to church three times every weekend:

Saturday night and twice on Sunday. And my face shows up regularly on video at our multisite campuses. But there's something more important going on in my mind—and in the minds of many others who show up weekly—than mere attendance. It's an understanding of why we attend and what we do once we leave.

And so, as I promised, I'll be sharing in this chapter some reasons I don't go to church anymore, and then we'll journey onward in the rest of this book to flesh out a more accurate definition of the church and how it is supposed to reflect the original character and agenda of God and his kingdom. That's something I've labored to teach and model for our church for many years now. It's catching on, but we have a long way to go.

Why I Don't Go to Church

1. Church isn't something you go to; it's something you are.

This goes back to the idea of completeness that we covered in chapter one. To be whole as a human being means to be reconnected to God from the spiritual estrangement brought on by sin. A human being who is still on the throne of his or her life is not only separated from God but is also incomplete. Just as the Father, Son, and Holy Spirit form the completion of the Godhead, a man or woman who surrenders his or her life back to God for him to rule finds completeness, or wholeness. It's what our first parents had before they sinned, and it's what made them whole and alive.

To live a life without God is to not be fully human. We exist, but we are not alive. We have breath, but we are dead in spirit. We work for a living, but our work is not fulfilling. We tend to exploit God's creation rather than help manage and conserve it. We're not alone in the world, but we're terribly lonely. We strive to get more, but we're never satisfied. We achieve many worldly trophies, but we're not being fruitful. And for all the woeful consequences that sin has brought to our lives and relationships, the most prolific and destructive impact of sin is our incompleteness.

Thankfully, salvation, beyond the normal implications of forgiveness and experiencing heaven when we die, is moreover a return to our original connectedness to God and its subsequent connectedness to others. It's why Jesus summed up a full and pleasing life as that where we love God with all our hearts and love others as ourselves. Relational and spiritual wholeness is the defining characteristic of God's original design for mankind—man created in his image (Image Dei)—and it brings wholeness to every other aspect of our real lives. It's what it means to be human. It's what it means to experience salvation. It's something you are, not something you go to. It's what it means to *be* the church.

2. Church isn't a place you go to; it's anywhere you go.

The word for "church" in the Bible is "*ecclesia*," and it is better described as "a gathering of people" than as "the place where people gather." The emphasis is on the people, not the place. God's kingdom cannot be confined geographically or contained physically. It's what happens in the hearts of people that counts—and then it's what happens with their feet. The church is everywhere the people with a heart for God are taken by their feet. The apostle Paul said as much when he cited the prophet Isaiah, as recorded in Romans 14:15: "How beautiful are the feet of the messengers who bring good news."

It's not that places are unimportant; God has always had a place for his people (e.g., the earth, the garden, the Promised Land, the place Jesus prepares for us so that we can be with him in John 14:2). But what makes those places the church, or the kingdom of God, is *who* is there and not *where* the place is. As Jesus said in Matthew 18:20, "Where two or three gather together as my followers, I am there among them." And even the promise in John 14 about preparing a place for us (which we always quantify as heaven) alludes to this: "There is more than enough room in my Father's home. If this were not so, would I have told you that I am going to prepare a place? When everything is ready, I will come and get you, so that you will always be with me where I am" (John 14:2, 3).

Did you see that? It's not so much that Jesus is preparing a *place* for us as it is that he wants us to be *with* him *wherever* he is. And isn't that what turned our first parents' paradise into problems? When they no longer were living in God's presence, they began living in a very different *place*, if for no other reason than that God wasn't there. Heaven, on the other hand, is chiefly characterized by the presence of God. Now, the church is far from being heaven, and we're definitely still in the "not yet" portion rather than the "already" portion of God's kingdom. But we'll talk more about that in a later chapter. For now, let us understand it as being anywhere we are with God's presence in us rather than somewhere we go hoping that he'll show up.

3. Church isn't something you go to; it's something you give to.

I probably don't need to mention that we live in a culture saturated with consumers. Even so (if it is indeed the case), I'm glad you purchased this book. There are times when being a consumer is right and necessary. Going to church is not one of those times. But honestly, a lot of people do go to church for what they get from it—or more as a consumer than a contributor.

Okay, before you jump all over me, I do realize that people can and do go to church to get help and guidance and inspiration. I'm certainly not saying this is a bad thing. But when you see the church only as something to *go to* rather than something *you are*, then it is easy to see it as more of a commodity than an identity. One of the ways you can recognize religious consumerism is to notice when a lot of people are coming to a building each weekend, but a very small percentage are sharing their lives in service to God and others at those services or during the rest of the week. I heard leadership guru John Maxwell once say that this kind of a church is like a professional football game, where sixty thousand people in desperate need of exercise are in the stands observing twenty-two men in desperate need of rest.

It's very difficult in a "What's in it for me?" culture to move people beyond going to church *services* and participating in the church *serving*. The Western church is particularly prone to this line of thinking. We go to church expecting a good return on our investment. We want the worship to be uplifting. We want the environment to be comfortable. We want the teaching to be inspiring. We want the vibe we get to be otherworldly. After all, we put our offering in the basket (maybe), and we deserve to get what we paid for. Okay, I know that sounds pretty crass, but how far from the truth is this, really, in the hearts and minds of many churchgoers? Did you notice how many times I used the phrase "We want" above?

People who are a part of a healthy church discover at some point that what it means to be the church is to live their lives the way Jesus lived his life. And if I could describe the life of Jesus in just one way, it would be that he was a *giver.* For all the things the incarnate Son of God could have demanded of his created kingdom (worship, acclaim, applause, recognition, being served), he lived the mantra he voiced: "It is more blessed to give than receive . . . For even the Son of Man came not to be served but to serve others and give his life as a ransom for many" (Acts 20:35; Matthew 20:28).

4. Church isn't a building you go to; it's something you build on.

Jesus said that *he* would build his church. It makes sense, then, that following Jesus, living by his power and according to his principles, and obeying his marching orders (the Great Commission and the Great Commandment) would be the prescription for *building* his church. And while holding weekend services in buildings has a place and purpose, it is a means and not an end.

People get hung up on the idea that for a church to be legitimate, it has to have a building. But the predominant idea in a kingdom is not houses and castles, but a king and his kingdom, which of course includes the people who live in his kingdom and under his rule. Does that include you?

It reminds me of the little rhyme we used to do in Sunday school. You remember saying it with folded hands, I'm sure: "This is the church. This is the steeple. Open the door and see all the people." That's very much a *go*-to-church mentality. So I've rewritten it to be more accurate: "This is a building. This is a steeple. If you're looking for church, then just look for the people." People who go to church often call their building the church. The church may meet in a building for one purpose or another, but the building is not the church. The people are.

5. Church isn't something you go to; it's a body of which you're a part.

This was the apostle Paul's favorite metaphor for the church. It's loaded with meaning, and it again points to something more organic than organizational. More identity than commodity. More community than individuality. In fact, everywhere Paul writes concerning believers in the church, he's using the second person plural. He's not referring to "you" in the singular when he addresses his audience. He's referring to "you" in the plural—in other words, "all of you." If he had been from the South, he would have used "Y'all." If he had been from the Bronx, he would have used "Youse guys." And if he had been from western Pennsylvania, as am I, he would certainly have uses "Y'uns." You know, "Y'uns are all a part of the church!"

Being the body of Christ also makes the point that Jesus is the head of his church. Bodies without heads—well, that's just morbid. I don't think I need to expound. But my point is that the vision, direction, and implementation strategy of the church come from the head alone. All the other parts of the body pull together and work according to their specific function for the body to be whole and effective. As with the building analogy, we see again the importance of our individual relationship with God through Christ and our corporate participation in his kingdom through community. The body of Christ isn't something you go to. It's something of which you are a part.

6. Church isn't something you go to; it's a family you belong to.

If the church is to reflect God's original template for his kingdom, then it must primarily pertain to relationships. The primary identity of the Christian is that he or she is a *child* of God. When we talk about our human families, we don't say, "I go to son" or "I go to daughter." We *are* sons of God. We *are* daughters of God. As fellow believers, we *are* brothers and sisters. And although this next group relates more to the mission of the church than her identity, even people who are far from God are children; they're just lost children who need to find their way back home. Being a part of a family is something you *are*. Therefore, it is more accurate to say, "I don't go to church; I am the church."

And when people say they are the church rather than saying they go to church, they are also indicating that they are a part of something bigger than just themselves. Remember that being made in the image of God also means being created for community. So while it's true enough to embrace the idea "I am the church," it is equally accurate, when speaking of the entire family of God, to say, "We are the church." But again, it's not something I go to or we go to; it's something I am and something we are.

One final thought here. This family is for everyone. I made an earlier remark about completeness and wholeness in God's image with reference to marriage and family. But what about those who aren't married, used to be married, have no children, or have only one parent? That's the beautiful thing about being the church. We become family for those who have no families—or really broken ones. Jesus made reference to this one day when his earthly family was trying to get to him through a crowd: "As Jesus was speaking to the crowd, his mother and brothers stood outside, asking to speak to him. Someone told Jesus, 'Your mother and your brothers are outside, and they want to speak to you.' Jesus asked, 'Who is my mother? Who are my brothers?' Then he pointed to his disciples and said, 'Look, these are my mother and brothers. Anyone who does the will of my Father in heaven is my brother and sister and mother!'" (Matthew 12:46–50).

So even people who find themselves outside the traditional contexts of marriage and family can still find spiritual wholeness in their relationship with Jesus and his extended family, the church. In fact, our family in Christ often becomes more of a source of love and support than our earthly families were ever capable of. So again, church isn't something you go to; it's a family you belong to.

Why You Shouldn't Go to Church

In the fall of 2007 I shared a series of messages with our church family, called "I Am the Church." Over the course of about seven weeks, I shared with them many of the concepts outlined in this book. It became an inspiration to many people's short-sighted perception of what church is really all about; and even better, it began to transform the way many of our folks began living out their daily lives. When they stopped *going* to church and started *being* the church—it helped *our* church become *the* church. I would make the same recommendation to you. You shouldn't go to church either. And if you don't, you'll discover what I (and what our people) discovered.

You'll use different language. You will catch yourself when you're about to say, "I'm going to church," and instead you'll realize you're simply going to a building to praise God, learn truth, serve in a ministry, or take a friend to experience a relevant (and, it is to be hoped, inspiring) message. You'll hear other people talking about going to church (meaning going to a church service) or going to the church (meaning the building with a steeple), and you'll be tempted to correct them. Maybe they'll be open to the teachable moment, but don't be surprised if they have no idea what you're talking about.

You'll expand your perimeter of ministry. You'll begin realizing that in being the church you're a minister like every other believer in your local church family. You'll find that it's not just the pastors and other paid leaders who do significant ministry. Their job (be they paid or volunteers) is to equip and resource other believers for their ministry. And you can use your spiritual gifts and human abilities everywhere you go—inside and outside the walls of the church. Every relationship is an opportunity to love in the name of Jesus, and every location is a missionary context. The church is like a Visa card; it's everywhere you want to be.

You'll realize everything is sacred. You will begin to notice that every act of kindness and opportunity to serve is yet another way to be the church. We even encourage people to share with us weekly in our church's communication links, describing to us how they were the church during that week. And it's amazing how our folks began to realize that being the church includes loving God and loving others no matter when or where one does it. We'll periodically share those stories to reinforce for others the comprehensive nature of being the church.

You can be the church when you're at church. You can be the church when you're at home. You can be the church when you're at work. You can be the church anywhere and everywhere you go. Therefore, everything is sacred. Everything is spiritual. And it's all being worked out in this real and present world, much in the way that Jesus modeled for us when he lived his earthly life and disclosed that the kingdom of heaven had drawn near.

You'll discover that you have some unlearning to do. This is especially true for those of us who grew up in the church. Before we can truly embrace all the implications and applications of being the church rather than going to church—we must unlearn the things that haven't gotten in the way of this revelation.

One of the most important principles toward this end has been in the Bible all along but has become lost (or at the very least muddied) over the centuries. I am speaking of the priesthood of the believer. There's a notion among many churchgoers that we pay the pastors to do the work of the church, and we'll come and cheer him or her on and do our best to fill the conventional Sunday morning roles and responsibilities all so we can have a nice service and go home until the next week. But the Bible says not only that every believer is a minister but also that every child of God is also a priest! The role of a priest is to bridge the gap between God and man. Jesus did that when God became a man. And believers in the church extend that mission as God's presence and proclaim God's message of good news.

Even Jesus understood his evangelistic limitations as just one man among the masses—and the potential for reaching the world if his Spirit were present in all those who would follow him. In one place he said, "I tell you the truth, anyone who believes in me will do the same works I have done, and even greater works, because I am going to be with the Father" (John 14:12).

It would only be in Jesus' leaving them and the subsequent arrival of the Holy Spirit that the church would continue the mission he began. Redemption had been accomplished, but the rejoining of people to a right relationship with God and to a restored humanity would continue. This would be the church's mandate in every culture and to every generation. And every believer—every follower of Christ—would have a part in that mission. It would necessitate the examination of every culture and each successive generation for the best possible way to reach them with the love of God and his message of reconciliation, or to strive for what the apostle Paul sets his sights on in 1 Corinthians 9:22–23 (NIV): "To the weak I became weak, to win the weak. I have become all things to all men so that by all possible means I might save some. I do all this for the sake of the gospel, that I may share in its blessings."

Paul was applying this comprehensive and customized plan not only to his own plans for sharing the gospel but also as a prescription for every believer—clergy and laity alike. So to unlearn what we've traditionally believed about pastors and laypersons, we'll have to consider some often-ignored truths about being the church.

That's what I'd like to deal with next.

CHAPTER 4

JUST CALL ME DAVE

> You are coming to Christ, who is the living cornerstone of God's temple. He was rejected by people, but he was chosen by God for great honor. And you are living stones that God is building into his spiritual temple. What's more, you are his holy *priests*. Through the mediation of Jesus Christ, you offer spiritual sacrifices that please God.
>
> —1 Peter 1:4–5, emphasis mine

I've always liked my name—Dave. But I've been called other things—some I probably shouldn't mention here. But then haven't we all? Most people call me Dave. It's casual and it's personal. But some people call me by my formal given name—David. My mom and dad call me David, and they always have. That's understandable. Most of my relatives call me David, with the notable exception of my uncles, who for some reason always called me Davey. And then there's my wife, Lori. She always calls me David. I don't ever remember an instance when she referred to me as Dave.

Occasionally, as a child and as a husband, my middle name has been included in instances of beckoning. "David Earl!" my mother would say. It was never a good thing when she had to use both first and middle names together. I mean, that's why we get middle names, right? Somewhere along the way my wife picked up on the attention-getting device as well, and when I'm not tuning in to her satisfaction, out comes the "David Earl."

More recently, and curiously, my dear wife has even begun to just call me Earl. I'm still trying to figure out what that is all about.

And though I've only ever heard it three or four times in my entire life, there's something riveting and threatening about hearing my name called out in triplicate: "David Earl Bish!" My immediate impulse upon hearing this has always been (and still is) to run and hide.

And then there are some of the other monikers that have been added over the years. I remember, as a brand-new schoolteacher, my delayed responses to being called Mr. Bish. To me, Mr. Bish was my dad. It was especially strange when one of my students saw me outside the context of the classroom—at the mall, for instance. They always seemed surprised to see me someplace other than the classroom. I was conditioned to hearing "Mr. Bish" in that context, but it took me a while to get used to it anywhere else.

Later on, after seminary and my first vocational ministry role, the prefix "Reverend" was added to Bish. I've never been comfortable with that one. It always seemed so formal. I grew more accustomed to the title "Pastor" and even more comfortable with "Pastor Dave." Years later, after we started Tri-County Church, one of the young guys who had started attending started calling me "P. D.," short for Pastor Dave. It took, and pretty soon a lot of folks were using that abbreviation for me. Some still do.

An Unhealthy Dichotomy

But I'll be honest, what I prefer most of all is when people simply call me Dave. I understand that my parents and my wife never will; I'm not sure I'd want them to. But Dave is what works best for me. And let me say sincerely that I'm not devaluing the roles of pastors or professional clergy in the least. I completely understand when people, out of respect for the office, feel the need to include "Reverend" or "Pastor" in front of my name. I never make a big deal whether they do or don't.

But here's what I think happens. When people hear or use those titles out of respect or habit, it can proliferate the perception that some people have a closer connection to God simply because of their position or what precedes their name. They may indeed have a close relationship with God, but it's not because of their position or title. I've noticed this mentality surface in some humorous ways, such as when I sometimes get blamed for inclement weather or someone asks me to put in a good word with the Big Man upstairs. I've even rebelled from acquiescing to the family Thanksgiving Dinner prayer in recent years. "You don't have to be a paid professional," I say in protest.

And so one weekend in the "I Am the Church" series I shared a message titled "Just Call Me Dave." The following week, I—along with the other pastors on our staff—symbolically changed our e-mail addresses by chopping off the "pastor" portion that preceded our first names. Mine went from pastordave@tricountychurch.net to just dave@ tricountychurch.net. It may seem like a simple gesture, but it was part of a larger strategy to begin dismantling the unhealthy dichotomy that exists in many churches, where the prevailing notion is that we pay the professionals to do the ministry and the only real spiritual wisdom that's available comes from the "sage on the stage." And I soon began to notice that we were beginning to gain some traction on the idea that *I am the church* wasn't just for Dave or the other pastors, but for every one of us who was following Jesus. *I* am the church. *You* are the church. *We* are the church.

Our Great High Priest

Those with an understanding of the Old Testament sacrificial system acknowledge the vital role of the priest in the Jewish religious culture. They were chosen from the tribe of Levi to superintend the regular and seasonal ceremonies, first in the nomadic days of the tabernacle and then later in temple worship. And of all the priests on the roster, there was one who stood out among them all—the high priest. And of all the ceremonies and observances, there was also one that towered in significance—the Day of Atonement.

Each year on the Day of Atonement, the high priest would enter the most sacred place (the Holy of Holies) and offer the annual sacrifice for the sins of all the people. This "blood of an innocent" sacrifice would *cover* the sins of the people for the previous year, necessitating that they return again the next year for the same purpose. The word "atonement" literally means "to cover." And that's just what the atoning sacrifice accomplished—*covering*.

Fast forward to the cross of Calvary, and Jesus would also take the position of a high priest—more specifically, our Great High Priest. Hebrews 5:1–3, 7–9 speaks of his role in this regard—and what sets him apart from every other high priest who preceded him:

Every high priest is a man chosen to represent other people in their dealings with God. He represents their gifts to God and offers sacrifices for their sins. And he is able to deal gently with ignorant and wayward people because he himself is subject to the same weaknesses. That is why he must offer sacrifices for his own sins as well as theirs . . . While Jesus was on the earth, he offered prayers and pleadings, with a loud cry and tears, to the one who could rescue him from death. And God heard his prayers because of his deep reverence for God. Even though Jesus was God's son, he learned obedience from the things he suffered. In this way God qualified him as a perfect High Priest, and he became the source of eternal salvation for all those who would obey him.

And so in Christ we have the Great High Priest, who has represented us before God. And what makes his representation so significant is that he didn't just *cover* our sins, as did all the other high priests who came before him, but he actually *took our sins away*. It was the full and final offering for sin, once and for all.

It went something like this: Jesus, as the perfect, sinless Son of God (akin to the unblemished Passover lamb) would fulfill the priestly role of being our representative to God by approaching God on sinful man's behalf. He would come to offer the sacrifice and purchase our forgiveness. But that's not the stunning part. Not only was Jesus the Great High Priest who would offer the sacrifice, but he himself was the sacrifice as well. The "blood of the innocent" would be his blood, making him both priest and sacrifice. Never had a high priest been able to offer so much—and never again would there be a need for a high priest to do so.

Now, having accomplished our forgiveness completely and satisfied the justice of God toward sin finally, the doorway is opened to this restored relationship with God and our reinstatement into his kingdom, for we would not only benefit from the luxurious and gracious gift of our Savior, but we would also be assigned our own priestly roles in his kingdom. "All glory to him who loves us and has freed us from our sins by shedding his blood for us. He has made us a *Kingdom of priests* for God his Father. All glory and power to him forever and ever! Amen" (Revelation 1:5–6, emphasis of mine).

Every Believer Is a Priest

This "priesthood of the believer" idea is not a new one. But like so many other biblical truths, it has been overlooked and underapplied. Thankfully, many preached messages and authored books have been raising this same awareness in recent days, and believers everywhere are recapturing the power and the joy of our indiscriminate calling as holy priests of God. This priesthood of the believer has several implications.

1. Everyone has the same advocate with God.

This is the unambiguous truth that the Scriptures point to in the person and work of Jesus Christ. Everyone has sinned against God, and there's no other remedy for our sin than the advocacy of Jesus, our Great High Priest. And it's only by believing in Jesus that anyone can appropriate this twofold reality of pardon and spiritual renewal. The resurrection is proof of the Advocate's successful defense on our behalf. When it comes to salvation, there's only no other way and there's no other name but Jesus.

2. Everyone has the same access to God.

This is one of the great realities in this idea of "I am the church." Every believer has as much potential for being with and learning from God as anyone else. We have the same Advocate, as we have already stated. We have the same Spirit who lives within those who believe. We have the same Word of God that his Holy Spirit uses to teach, encourage, and correct us. And we have the same expectation that God will receive us as an equal-opportunity recipient of this care and attention. I think you'll agree with me that what God says in Hebrews 4:14–16 makes this clear: "So then, since we have a great High Priest who has entered heaven, Jesus the Son of God, let us hold firmly to what we believe. This High Priest of ours understands our weaknesses, for he faced all of the same testings we do, yet he did not sin. So let us come boldly to the throne of our gracious God. There we will receive his mercy, and we will find grace to help us when we need it most."

Our confidence to approach God in our weaknesses is guaranteed by Jesus being able to pass every test we failed. Again, it's Jesus that puts us all on a level playing field as our advocate and our access. But there's one more implication of being a kingdom of priests.

3. Everyone has the same assignment from God.

This third idea is where being the church really comes into play. God calls every believer in his Son to carry on the reconciliatory mission of his Son as well. I don't mean by this that we bring about anyone else's redemption; that was done once and for all by the Great High Priest. What I do mean is that with Christ dwelling in us through the Holy Spirit, we become the presence of God in the world and carry on the same ambassadorial role our Old Testament counterparts had when they, too, were to represent and introduce the one true God to the world he created.

"Living" Stones

Consider the implications in 1 Peter 2:5: "And you are living stones that God is building into his holy temple. What's more, you are his holy priests. Through the mediation of Jesus Christ, you offer spiritual sacrifices that please God." In an amazing parallel to Jesus' comprehensive role as the visible presence of God, the Great High Priest to God, and the acceptable sacrifice for God—we too, as the church, carry on these roles as well, albeit to a lesser degree.

So believers in Christ are not just *subjects* in God's kingdom; we're the temple—the dwelling place of God. And we're not just the temple of the living God; we're priests, representing God to others. And we're not just priests of God; we're sacrifices too—make that "living" sacrifices. Our sacrifices aren't for the purpose of redemption, but for the sake of others recognizing their need for it. When we sacrifice, or give away, our lives for the sake of others, they too may be awakened to God's love for them and the kind of life God originally intended for them to live. Let's take a closer look at these three "living" manifestations of the presence of God in the world—or, again, what it means to *be* the church.

A "Living" Temple

Jesus was unquestionably referring to himself as the temple of God when he said it would be torn down and rebuilt in three days. He was the walking, talking, visible presence of God in the world—the Word made flesh. Likewise, those who would follow him and be filled with his Spirit on the Day of Pentecost would also become the walking, talking, visible dwelling of God in the world. It's still true today. We are the body of Christ. We are the living temple.

"Holy" Priests

Jesus was also the Great High Priest, as we have said. With the indwelling of the Holy Spirit, every believer would also take on the priestly responsibility of mediating between God and those who are still far from him. This is not in the same sense as Jesus' redemptive mediation, but as representatives. Those who know God and have a relationship with him have the privilege and the responsibility to share this opportunity with others. This was symbolized in the rending of the veiled entrance to the Holy of Holies—access to God from both directions. In this regard, Abraham could be considered the precursor to the office of priest. Walking by faith in God as Abraham did, we too become holy priests.

"Living" Sacrifices

Finally, Jesus was the first of a long line of living sacrifices. It would be his death and return to life that would serve as the precedent for all people of faith (past, present, and future) to experience freedom from death's penalty and a return to life as God originally intended. Every other animal sacrifice in the past died and stayed dead. Jesus, the once-and-for-all sacrifice, would die and be resurrected. And those who would follow Jesus by faith in the future would not only benefit from this forgiveness and new life in the Spirit, but would also willingly and gratefully offer their lives back to God as living sacrifices. You may already be familiar with this: "And so, dear brothers and sisters, I plead with you to give your bodies to God because of all he has done for you. Let them be a living and holy sacrifice—the kind he will find acceptable. This is truly the way to worship him" (Romans 12:1).

In other words, the church of Jesus becomes the vehicle for the increasingly visible resurgence of God's kingdom on this earth. And the church is composed of everyone who has surrendered the reigns of life to follow Jesus and, through the power of the Holy Spirit, live a transformed life that illustrates the character of God in human form. This comprehensive and redemptive purpose of forgiveness, new life, and mission is summed up quite nicely by the expression, "Jesus gave his life *for* you, so he could give his life *to* you, so he could live his life *through* you."

"Living" Lights

Jesus couched this present reality with the words "salt" and "light," meaning that we would have an impact on others based on our reflection of him and our proximity to them. They would experience God's presence in the way we live and be drawn to his goodness. You can see this surely in the following passage:

> You are the salt of the earth. But what good is salt if it has lost its flavor? Can you make it salty again? It will be thrown out and trampled underfoot as worthless. You are the light of the world—like a city on a hilltop that cannot be hidden. No one lights a lamp and then puts it under a basket. Instead, a lamp is placed on a stand, where it gives light to everyone in the house. In the same way, let your good deeds shine out for all to see, so that everyone will praise your heavenly Father. (Matthew 5:13–16)

The apostle Peter also contrasts those who don't recognize the honor that belongs to Christ in this regard with those who do when he writes, "But you are not like that, for you are a chosen people. You are royal priests, a holy nation, God's very own possession. As a result, you can show others the goodness of God, for he called you out of the darkness into his wonderful light" (1 Peter 1:9).

All these passages are in reference to every believer, not just reverends and pastors and missionaries in the classical sense. We may all have different roles and gifts, but we are all saved and called by the same name—Jesus. And so if you're a follower of Christ, you're a priest, whether you have a title in front of your name or not, whether you've been to seminary or not, and whether you get paid in ministry or not. This is why I love it when people just call me Dave.

Celebrity Church

As is the case with so many other places in our culture, we have become infatuated with high-profile personalities and renowned practitioners. Take nothing away from the giftedness and impact of many of these fellow priests in the kingdom of God; I admire many of them and have benefitted from their inspiration and example. But the same thing happens in wider ministry arenas in the local church. We feel so overwhelmed by the things God is doing in other places and through other people that we create another dichotomy of elitism. And I get the impression that many of these leaders would shudder to think that anyone might view them as anything more than a colaborer in the church at large.

Paul, the apostle, had to handle a similar "My pastor's better than your pastor" saga in his ministry. It was then as it is now, with people lining up behind their spiritual champion. Paul pointed out how much like the world their behavior was: "When one of you says, 'I am a follower of Paul,' and another says, 'I follow Apollos,' aren't you acting just like people of the world? After all, who is Apollos? Who is Paul? We are only God's servants through whom you believed the Good News. Each of us did the work the Lord gave us. I planted the seed in your hearts, and Apollos watered it, but it was God who made it grow" (1 Corinthians 3:4–6).

But there are still a great number of church leaders and churchgoers that hold on to these perceptions. And some even like it. In our humanness, those of us with titles in front of our name (credentialed or not) have our egos stroked when people address us this way. We secretly enjoy being needed by people, and we hide our disappointment when someone finds equally helpful advice from a noncredentialed source. As church leaders, we need to change our thinking of this and realize that it's not healthy for us or our people.

People without titles can prefer this too. Like so many who grew up in a church culture in which the pastor did all the significant ministry (preaching, teaching, counseling, visiting the sick and imprisoned, etc.), they not only expect it to continue that way, but they also find that it's, well, just easier. But both the pastors who relish this and the parishioners who expect it are missing out on the blessings of the priesthood.

Equipping the Saints

I'd like to offer one more observation before I bring this chapter to a close. Most of us are familiar with the verses in Ephesians 4 that enumerate the various offices and ministry roles within the church. Let me refresh your memory: "Now these are the gifts Christ gave to the church: the apostles, the prophets, the evangelists, and the pastors and teachers. Their responsibility is to equip God's people to do his work and build up the church, the body of Christ. This will continue until we all come to such unity in our faith and knowledge of God's Son that we will be mature in the Lord, measuring up to the full and complete standard of Christ" (Ephesians 4:11–13).

Now I'm guessing that you (as I did for a long time) understand these various job titles to be akin to the modern-day church's paid professionals. But these wonderful equipping gifts are not necessarily paid church staff personnel. I'm pretty sure they didn't even have such paid staff at this point in the early church's development, and as we know, many like the apostle Paul were bi-vocational or fully self-supported.

The fact is that there are many people in our churches who have the equipping gifts enumerated in this passage and yet are not called to full-time paid ministry. They can, however, effectively fulfill ministry roles within and outside our church walls that help others to discover and be trained for their place in ministry. They can work quite successfully alongside other staff and volunteers to lead and equip. Most of them are already doing it successfully in the marketplace and, quite frankly, are able to do a much better job than many who attempt to do it as paid professionals in the church.

Let me emphasize that I'm not belittling the need for those who serve on the staffs of churches. I am one of those I speak of, and I could not hope to lead our church in the mission God has given us without the great people on our staff that I work with every day. I am thankful that they embrace, as I do, the concept that people with equipping and leadership gifts need to find their places of service in the church or out in the community, and that they are just as much a full-time minister as Pastor So-and-So or Reverend Such-and-Such.

And I really love watching this happen in our church and community. Every once in a while, someone will greet me with "Hey Pastor D . . . Sorry, I mean, Dave." I smile and tell them not to worry about it. But it's really cool when they catch themselves and really understand why I want them to just call me Dave.

CHAPTER 5

JESUS NEVER SAID TO GO WITNESSING

> So when the apostles were with Jesus, they kept asking him, "Lord, has the time come for you to free Israel and restore our kingdom?" He replied, "The Father alone has the authority to set those dates and times, and they are not for you to know. But you will receive power when the Holy Spirit comes upon you. And you will *be* my witnesses, telling people about me everywhere—in Jerusalem, throughout Judea, in Samaria, and to the ends of the earth."
>
> —Acts 1:6–8, emphasis mine

I really wasn't looking forward to doing it, but I knew that, if I really was a Christian, I had to. I had to go witnessing. A group of us was going to spread out over the downtown area where we lived and just go around looking for people with whom we could share the gospel. The thought hadn't crossed my mind how I would actually do that—how I would approach people or how I would initiate the conversation. I guess I'm admitting that we hadn't received adequate training for our mission.

And while that was true, I'm not sure our effectiveness quotient would have been any better even if we had received adequate training. But we were going. We were going witnessing. Because this is what Jesus told his disciples to do.

Or did he?

I need to say right off that I'm not against doing evangelism this way or criticizing those who do. I'm just not sure that it's very effective, or that it's a biblical model. More importantly, I don't think Jesus ever said we were to do it. If you take a closer look at the Scripture in Acts chapter one, cited at the beginning of this chapter, you'll notice that what Jesus actually said to his disciples was, ". . . and you will *be* my witnesses . . . telling people about me everywhere" (italics mine). He didn't say *go* witnessing. He said *be my* witnesses. So in the same way that church isn't something you go to, it's something you are. Likewise, witnessing isn't something you do; it's also something you are. It's an identity, not a strategy.

Having teased you with the opening, you may be wondering how my "witnessing" experience panned out. Well, one guy I approached had just come out of a bar (that should have been warning to me), and when I asked if I could share something important with him, he said, grunting out his words, "I'm tired, I'm hungry, and I'm going home." I'm guessing tired and hungry wasn't all he "was," but he didn't give me time to assess how much influence the tavern time had on him.

I approached a few others who responded with similar indifference. Some were more polite than others, but I didn't have much progress or success. I was about ready to call it quits. As I was walking back to my car, I caught sight of a man coming in my direction in the parking lot and I gave it one more shot. I asked him if he had a moment and told him that I'd like to share something important with him. I was fully ready for his dismissal and was already mentally preparing for my journey home when he said, "Really? You have something that's so important that you want to talk to someone you don't even know?"

"Well, yes," I said, halfway mumbling, "as a matter of fact I do."

I don't honestly remember what all I shared with this guy after that, but I do remember his response. And before you presume the best-case scenario, he didn't fall to his knees and ask what he had to do to get saved. Rather, he looked at me and he said, "You really believe this, don't you?"

"Yes," I said, "I really do."

"Well, I believe that you believe this, young man, and I'm very impressed that you do so enough to talk to total strangers. I'm not really convinced of anything you've said to me, but I'm glad for you, and for your beliefs." And then he walked away.

I have to say that on this occasion and several others in my life where this strategy was in play, I've had the same impression. It was very difficult. It seemed unnatural. And it wasn't very effective. It wasn't even the rejections that bothered me as much as the indifference. And honestly, at the end of the day, I want what Christ has done in my life and the vital message of the gospel to make a difference. I don't want to feel good about others believing I believe in Jesus. I want them to want to believe in Jesus for themselves.

I guess what I'm really saying is that there's something else I believe in. I believe that Jesus never told his followers to *go* witnessing. I believe he told them to *be* witnesses, and that in doing so they would have a powerful impact on those who witnessed their, well, *being* witnesses. So in the same vein as our discussion in chapter two, *being* the church as opposed to *going* to church applies to our witness in this world for Christ. Witnessing is something you *are*, not something you *do*.

The Message of the Witnesses

Sometimes we learn to associate certain people with the thing they are most passionate about. One would easily conclude that the message Mother Teresa gave witness to was that of compassion. Dr. Martin Luther King's life message was a social justice predicated upon divine human rights. His life was a witness to that far more than the eloquent words he used to describe it. Both of their life messages were expressions of a more holistic message, the message of Jesus—what we often refer to as the good news. And they were witnesses to that message.

But no one brought that message of the good news to bear the way Jesus did. He is referred to in the prologue to the gospel of John as the "message," or the logos of God. In other words, he didn't come into the world just to bring the message or preach the message; he was (and is) the message: "In the beginning the Word already existed. The Word was with God, and the Word was God. He existed in the beginning with God.

God created everything through him, and nothing was created except through him. The Word gave life to everything that was created, and his life brought light to everyone" (John 1:1–40).

There's a similar (albeit more diffused) sense in which we as believers in Christ also embody the message of the good news—much as I referred to earlier in the examples of Mother Teresa and Martin Luther King. We certainly do not do so to the degree that Jesus did as God incarnate, but in a lesser way, in which we reflect the character of Christ as we walk in our new life in the Spirit and tell others about him. This is why John the Baptist was described not as the light himself, but as simply a witness to the light whom everyone might believe because of his testimony. (See John 1:6–8). It's also why the early followers of Jesus were called Christians (meaning "little Christs"), or followers of the Way, referring to the fact that they lived their lives the way Jesus lived his.

What is apparent is that their expression of the message of Jesus was not limited to speeches and conversations about right theology or how to get to heaven. Rather, it was manifested in a life lived in humble service to others that was driven by their love for God. Jesus did indeed instruct them to "tell people about me everywhere," but it was in the context of first "being" witnesses. What better way is there to illustrate to someone the message and character of Jesus than to be a walking, talking example of what he himself lived out? Incidentally, we do this better in community than we do in isolation. That's because we're his body, and our corporate relationships make the body more complete. And those relationships are the context of our witness.

The Context of the Witnesses

Another implication of the mandate in Acts 1 is that being a witness is always carried out in a relational context. I believe that relational context has three categories. There's the relationship with the one you're being a witness of—Jesus, of course. Then there are the relationships you have with the other witnesses. And finally, there are the relationships with those to whom you are being a witness. If that sounds confusing to you, let's break it down.

The starting point for being a witness of Christ is an authentic and intimate personal relationship with Jesus. You have surrendered your life to follow him, you're living a life submitted to the Holy Spirit, who lives within you, and you spend time regularly with him in his Word for the purpose of simply being with God. Yes, you learn about God and what God may expect of you, but it's primarily for the purpose of being in his presence with humility and submission. It's the time you spend growing in your intimacy with God that reveals how much greater he is than you ever imagined and how much you need his grace and power to live as someone who reflects his character and glory.

But the character of God is always manifested in the context of community, just as God himself, in his completeness and unity, is community (e.g. Father, Son, and Holy Spirit). So reflecting the character of Jesus in love and service has to have an object of that loving and serving. It's not in the spirit of what Jesus told his disciples to merely go running about all over the countryside, simply telling people things about Jesus, although the truth about his death, resurrection, and ascension are compelling and necessary elements of the gospel. Rather, the disciples were to have the significant details of his divinity and payment for sin accompanied by the transformative power of the Spirit in their own lives as they cared for and sacrificed for others the way Jesus did.

The primary context for this loving life of servitude was the family—both the real families they were a part of and the church family they had been incorporated into. It was a common observation among the people who were not a part of the believing community that these Christians didn't live for themselves the way others did. And Jesus himself said that others would know that they were his followers by their love for one another: "By this all men will know that you are my disciples, if you love one another" (John 13:35).

There was something quite compelling about this community of people who lived together and took care of each other in unselfish ways. Onlookers would have found it not just intriguing, but also difficult to believe, that people would share what they had with each other instead of constantly looking out for their own needs. Keep in mind there were no social services in those days to meet the needs of marginalized and disenfranchised people. Nor was there socialism, where one didn't have a choice but to share. They did it because they loved God and each other. And they didn't show this love just to those inside their group. They expressed it to those on the outside as well. You might conclude that genuine Christianity is as beneficial to those who aren't followers of Jesus as it is to those who are.

Speaking of those on the outside, this final context of being a witness is what most of us think about when the idea of witnessing comes to mind. We've mentioned the primary relationship with Jesus himself, and the relationship fellow believers had with one another, both of which establish a fundamental witness of Jesus and his good news. But now, in the classic sense of evangelism, there are the relationships we have with people who are not yet a part of God's family. Remember what Jesus said: "You will be my witnesses, telling people about me everywhere—in Jerusalem, throughout Judea, in Samaria, and to the ends of the earth" (Acts 1:8).

Telling people about Jesus everywhere we go is certainly an important aspect of evangelism—and of being a witness of Christ. The apostle Paul writes about it in Romans when he says, "How beautiful are the feet of messengers who bring good news" (10:15). In those days, if you went anywhere, you traveled by foot. So Paul is saying that everywhere your feet take you is an opportunity to share the good news of Jesus in action and in speech.

And again we see how vital the precedent of being a witness is to the actual telling to people about Jesus. Living out the character of Christ and the agenda of God's kingdom is a prerequisite to explaining the mechanics of becoming a Christian. Traditionally we have placed a lot of emphasis on people understanding the doctrine of salvation and praying a sinner's prayer as a sign of commitment, both of which have validity in this discussion. But if we have not established a relationship with the people we're sharing Christ with and haven't had the opportunity to love and care for them the way Jesus would (and does), then it comes off as more of a sales pitch than it does the power of God unto salvation. Many Christians are quick to share the plan of salvation with others but are far less concerned with whether the way they are living their life and the way they are treating people is a witness to the way Jesus lived his life.

We are compelled, then, to tell people everywhere about Jesus not so they can go to heaven when they die, but to share with them the opportunity to live as God always intended them to live—with a life of grace and forgiveness, redemption and justice, love and fulfillment; a life that can only be experienced by surrendering to God and receiving his gift of new life. And it's a whole lot easier to see what that new life looks like when the person telling you about it has experienced it for himself or herself.

So where are these people?

The Range of the Witnesses

The idea of being witnesses everywhere seems a little daunting. But here again, Jesus isn't assuming that just one person, or even a few, would be engaging in this endeavor. It would be many people living out lives of love and service toward each other and those they met along the way. In fact, when Jesus told his disciples that they would do greater works than even he did ("I tell you the truth, anyone who believes in me will do the same *works* I have done, and even *greater works,* because I am going to be with the Father" [John 14:12, emphasis mine]), I believe he meant that the exponential potential of the church to expand, with every believer becoming a witness to the person and message of Jesus, would accomplish much more kingdom advancement than he could do as one man walking the earth—even though that one man was also God in the flesh.

He told them to be his witness in Jerusalem, in Judea, to Samaria, and to the ends of the earth. He didn't mean in one day. But he was giving them a hint at his strategy. They would begin where they were, Jerusalem, and as their influence grew and more people began following Christ and being discipled as they themselves had been, the territory would expand. There would certainly be strategic and intentional plans to connect with people and teach about Jesus; the book of Acts records that gathering for the apostles' teaching, fellowship, breaking bread, and prayer were core values. But it would in large part be a result of them living their lives together as a community of people following and becoming more like Jesus. And the changes that were happening in the way they were living their lives was contagious.

What was transpiring in Jerusalem would spread to the surrounding region of Judea. And from Judea it would spread to those outside the circle of their cultural and religious identity, Samaria. And then from Samaria, with an ever-increasing momentum, it would spread to the rest of the planet. When I read Acts 1:8 in the past, I thought it was just one person who traveled a lot, rather than the progressive consequences of relational discipleship. The same issue occurs when we see the Great Commission "go into all the world and make disciples" as referring to travel to somewhere else in the world, rather than what I think Jesus was really implying—namely, making disciples while going along in the world.

Likewise, we are called to begin to follow the way of Christ in our families and in our neighborhoods where we are. And as others embrace the forgiveness of God and the way of love exemplified in Jesus, the expansion continues. We begin to reach out to those on the margins and those who are not like us (Samaritans). All of this comes with a commitment to the perpetual nature of making disciples who make disciples rather than just converting them. This is what Jesus told us to do in order to fulfill his original intent for going into the world.

This is amazing to ponder, and we've discussed the significance of Jesus' earthly mission in the opening chapters. But while his mission on earth was primarily to offer himself as the sacrifice for all sin, he would entrust the mission and message of worldwide reconciliation into the hands of his followers. Jesus did what was necessary so that we could be saved, but those who would follow him and bear witness to him would carry the life-transforming power and truth of the gospel forward. They (and we) would *be* his witnesses.

It's also in this opening chapter of the book of Acts that we read about Jesus' ascension into heaven. It seems strange and even careless to leave the disciples on their own at such a critical time in the mission. But Jesus had accomplished what he had come to earth to do, and he had spent three years preparing and apprenticing his team to carry on the next phase of the mission. So he didn't leave them unprepared, and he wasn't about to leave them unempowered.

The Power of the Witnesses

Immediately prior to Jesus telling his disciples that they would be his witnesses, he says this: "But you will receive power when the Holy Spirit comes upon you" (Acts 1:8). It is not without reason that Jesus makes this statement as a prerequisite to his marching orders. Essentially, it is impossible to be a witness for Christ—especially if we define being a witness as living the kind of life Jesus lived—without the indwelling power of the Holy Spirit. The power he speaks of doesn't refer to their plans, strategies, and boldness for spreading the gospel as much as it does to the transformation of their lives as Christ followers and the impact their Christlikeness will have on others. So important was this prerequisite that he warns them to not to do anything or go anywhere (e.g., tarry in Jerusalem) until this powerful element of the mission was given to them.

We of course discover this in the second chapter of Acts, where the record of the Holy Spirit's arrival takes place. They were meeting in the upper room, and a rushing wind and tongues of fire filled not just the room but also the believers themselves. What would follow were lives lived in complete devotion to Christ, in commitment to one another, and with a passion to share the love of God with others, as witnessed in the reality of radically transformed lives. Thus it would not simply be their declarations about Jesus—his divinity, his death, his resurrection, etc.—that would compel others to follow, but the evidence that others would see in how God had changed their lives.

Finally, people would witness authentic examples (not perfect examples) of the heart of God living inside the hearts of people. Unlike the religious leaders and their toxic combination of self-righteousness, hypocrisy, and condemnation, these believers in Jesus, these followers of the Way, were illustrations of how God desires to be a part of every person's life, and that this leads to a loving relationship and not a life of impossible rules and a façade of rituals.

One interesting anecdote of the Holy Spirit's commencement in the lives of the early believers was the supernatural manifestation of speaking in tongues. We often get caught up in the miraculous nature of this event (and I'm not saying we shouldn't, necessarily; it's an awesome thing), but I think there's some merit in recognizing its purpose with respect to the mission Jesus gives his followers. Acts 2:4 says, "And everyone present was filled with the Holy Spirit and began speaking in other languages, as the Holy Spirit gave them this ability." It just so happened (okay, not just so, but purposely so) that there were Jews from every nation of the world living in or staying in Jerusalem at that time, and they all heard the believers telling them the good news about Jesus in their native tongues and dialects. In other words, among the three thousand people who became followers of Christ on that single day, many of them would take this good news along with their changed lives back to their homelands. Somehow the spread of the good news to Jerusalem, Judea, Samaria, and the rest of the world doesn't seem so unrealistic now.

But the power of the witnesses wasn't limited to the miracle of speaking in unknown and unlearned languages. We read of many other miracles attributed to the apostles as their ministry authority is authenticated and those witnessing their teaching and wondrous signs recognize God's power is in them. But the grandest miracle of all was seen in the way these followers of Jesus were living their lives. A little later, in Acts chapter 4:32–34, we read, "All the believers were united in heart and mind. And they felt that what they owned was not their own, so they shared everything they had. The apostles testified powerfully to the resurrection of the Lord Jesus, and God's great blessing was upon them all. There were no needy people among them, because those who owned land or houses would sell them and bring the money to the apostles to give to those in need."

What really amazed people were the daily miracles that were taking place in the lives of those who had gone from living for themselves to living for God and for others. How else can you explain the transformation from a selfish life to a selfless one? As we allow Christ to transform us into the kind of people who love and give and share and forgive, it establishes a powerful witness to the person and power of Jesus. And it validates everything we might or should say about him specifically. Our changed lives are what make us such an effective witness to Christ. It was no less of a miracle than healing people or speaking in tongues in Acts chapter two. And it is no less than a miracle when it happens today. And it does happen today. It happens when someone decides to follow Jesus and become his disciple.

It's true, then, that Jesus never said to go witnessing.

But he did say, "Follow Me."

CHAPTER 6

FOLLOW ME

> One day as Jesus was walking along the shore of the Sea of Galilee, he saw two brothers—Simon, also called Peter, and Andrew—throwing a net into the water, for they fished for a living. Jesus called out to them, "Come, follow me, and I will show you how to fish for people!" And they left their nets at once and followed him.
>
> —Matthew 4:18–20

Like any man, I have a tough time stopping to ask for directions, but on this day I was short on time and had to go against my instincts. I was actually stopping by our local Wal-Mart to grab something for my daughter. So instead of my usual pursuit as a hunter-gatherer, I made straight away for the nearest blue-smock-wearing employee and asked where I might find the item in question. "Well, it's just over—" She stopped midsentence to switch gears. Then she began again with, "I know exactly where it is. Why don't you follow me?"

And so I did. She in fact did know where she was going, and I had the item in my hand in a matter of moments. I sincerely thanked my hunting guide and was soon on my way out the door. I was thinking as I was driving away that life would be a much easier enterprise if we always had someone to lead us to where we need to be. Not just someone shouting out directions or drawing us a map, but someone who says, "I know exactly where you need to go. Follow me." You probably know where I'm going with this.

There's something fascinating about looking at some of the things Jesus didn't say, as we've been doing so far in this book. Jesus never told his disciples to go to church. He never told his disciples to go witnessing. Come to think of it, he never told them to start a religion, be good people, or make a difference in the world. And he certainly never told them to study him. He simply said, "Follow me." As simple as that invitation may sound, it contains everything we need to know about being a Christian. Let me say something about that to start.

I have grown more and more uncomfortable with the label "Christian" over the years. It's not that I'm ashamed of the term or that I don't believe with all my heart that I am, in fact, a Christian. It's just that the term itself can mean so many things to so many people. And it's not the plethora of definitions within the religious sector that I'm as concerned about as the pejorative term it has become among irreligious people. Not that being a Christian is supposed to be popular or unmet with any cultural or spiritual resistance, but the term often carries many unnecessary stigmas that have been perpetuated by people who claim to be Christians but don't very much resemble Christ. It was Gandhi who said, "You Christians don't look very much like your Christ."

This unfortunate theme is also the subject of some recent writings that have helped shape some of my perspective. Dan Kimball's *They Like Jesus But Not the Church* and Gabe Lyon's *unChristian* are two that I would highly recommend. Both volumes point out with genuine anecdotal evidence that many people are disillusioned with religion and church but are still intrigued by the person and life of Jesus Christ. And so, if we're to be the kind of effective "witnesses" of Jesus that we know he calls us to be, it is imperative that we in fact look and act like the Jesus that many people are still interested in knowing more about.

So, for my liking, the better expression is Christ follower. When people ask me, or if I'm trying to share my worldview, I prefer to say, "I'm a Christ-follower" or a "I'm a follower of Jesus," as opposed to saying, "I'm a Christian." The only reason I take the time for this clarification is that with so much at stake, eternally speaking, I believe we need to get this idea right in our own hearts and minds before we attempt to bring others into the deal. If we really *are* the church and not just *going*, and if we really are *witnesses* and not just *witnessing*, and if we really are following Jesus and not just Christians, then I think our impact on those who are still far from God will not only be effective but will also be accompanied by the very power and influence of Christ himself.

So with that, let's talk some more about what it means to follow Jesus.

Drop What You're Doing

Jesus' invitation to Peter and Andrew was simple and direct. He simply said, "Come, follow me, and I will show you how to fish for people!" What amazes me about this passage is that Peter and Andrew left their nets at once and followed him. The very same thing happens a little while later on the same beach when Jesus offers the same invitation to James and John:

A little farther up the shore, he saw two other brothers, James and John, sitting in a boat with their father, Zebedee, repairing their nets. And he called them to come, too. They immediately followed him, leaving the boat and their father behind. (See Matthew 4:21–22.)

Do you find it as shocking as I do that they would completely walk off the job (and the family business, in the case of the sons of Zebedee) and go with some religious itinerant that they had never even met before? It kind of reminds me of the way Abraham packed up and left his country when God simply said, "Hey Abe, I want you to move!" What was so compelling and irresistible about Jesus that they would drop what they were doing to follow him?

Well, a couple of things come to mind. First, I am quite certain that even if these fishing buddies had never met Jesus, they had most likely heard about him. Many rabbis came and went, but Jesus was different. He wasn't like the other religious leaders who treated the common people with criticism and condescension. He was a man of the people, and his words rang with the truth of freedom and restoration. Not to mention that the miraculous signs he was performing were causing quite a stir as well.

But what must have amazed Peter, Andrew, James, and John more than anything was that Jesus, a rabbi, was inviting them to become his disciples. They were fishermen, for crying out loud. Rabbis never called simple, uneducated, blue-collar fishermen to be their disciples. This honor was only for the most respected, well-educated, prestigious Jewish families with young sons of promise. The guys Jesus chose had no such pedigree. Their rabbinical résumés were laughable, and besides that, they smelled like fish.

While they might have been enamored with the thought of being students of a rabbi and jumped at the opportunity, I think something much more significant is in play here. It has to do with Jesus' obvious reference to their transition from fishing for fish to fishing for men. Here's what I imagine is going on in their minds. On more than one occasion, on the dusty road home from a long day of fishing, the conversation turns to the realization and the question that there has to be something more to life than getting up, going to work, and coming home, simply to do it all over again the next day. They were looking for more. It's a conversation most of us have had. It simply goes like this: "There's got to be more."

And Jesus is not saying that a job in vocational ministry is any more fulfilling than being a self-employed fisherman. In fact, professional preaching can be just as tedious and distracting to what it means to follow Jesus as any other profession. Believe me; I know. What Jesus was really inviting them to was the more—the more they were looking for. There is more, according to Jesus. And we find it when we follow him.

There are three things we must keep in mind as we examine the call of these disciples to follow Jesus. First, the invitation is open to everyone, regardless of station or stature. Second, the operative word is "follow." Jesus is simply asking them to follow. No prerequisites; no prequalifications. Just drop what you're doing and follow. And third—and most significantly—his invitation to all was to follow *him*. The most important aspect is that what (or who, I should say) we're following is Jesus. We'll take a closer look at each of these components.

Come Unto Me

Nobody other than Jesus better understands how much we're all looking for more. God in fact created us for himself, so he knows that as long as we choose or follow something or someone else, we'll always be looking for more. It's how this whole sin thing got started in the first place. Adam and Eve were deceived into thinking there was something more than God, and God gave them (as he does all of us) the choice to go after it. We all know how that ended. But the beauty of the gospel of Jesus is that, in the finished work of the cross and the gift of new life in the Spirit, we can choose to come back to the only thing that can satisfy us completely—God!

Realizing the hopelessness and weariness of a life without God—and even more, a religious life without God—Jesus offers this invitation in Matthew 11:28–30: "Come unto me, all of you who are weary and carry heavy burdens, and I will give you rest. Take my yoke upon you. Let me teach you, because I am humble and gentle at heart, and you will find rest for your souls. For my yoke is easy to bear, and the burden I give you is light."

Do you see it? The invitation to come is open to everyone—all who are weary and burdened. I believe there's a twofold application to Jesus' invitation. The first part is the general way in which we all find life to be wearisome and unfulfilling. Not that every day is a bummer, but if you're honest, there are only so many things you can have and only so many experiences to try. And at the end of the day, you have to get more and try more in order to stay fulfilled. Jesus is inviting us to the more that satisfies.

The second aspect of Jesus' invitation, as I see it, has to do with the burden of the existing religious structures and mandates. Living up to the law of God, as the Pharisees so clearly instructed (but couldn't live up to themselves), was truly a wearisome exercise. Jesus was also inviting everyone to be free of that as well. It's like he's pointing out that for all their religious commitment and fervor, they're not really happy after all. What's more, it feels more like a burden than a blessing.

What Jesus offers, then, in replacement of the endless cycle of weariness, is what every weary person needs most of all—rest. He doesn't tell them to try harder. He essentially tells them to give up. And the reason they (and we) can give up is that Jesus fulfills the requirement of the law in the living of a perfect life, and he offers us the power and refreshment of that new life in the Spirit—his Spirit, which is living in us. We receive that when we surrender our lives to follow him. Jesus is saying that what we really need and what we're really looking for is him. We do that by taking his yoke upon us, which is another way of following Jesus in an intimately connected way.

The Yoke's On You

A yoke metaphor wouldn't have been lost on Jesus' original audience, but it may be helpful for us to have some clarification. A yoke is a double harness of sorts that two animals, or beasts of burden, would be coupled to in a side-by-side fashion. The notion that two is better than one certainly applies to primitive agricultural fieldwork, but it is even more relevant as it relates to following Jesus. Jesus asks us to follow not just in a "hope you can keep up" kind of way, but in such a way that we are inextricably linked to him in this spiritual relationship. We are spiritually connected to Jesus and are walking with him side by side.

In most cases you would imagine the optimum paring of animals in a yoke to be two of equal strength. But often, a younger, less strong, and less mature animal would be yoked with a seasoned veteran of the plow. While it may seem unfair to the beast with seniority, it served the purpose of helping the new recruit learn the ropes—literally. And in time the younger would understand what the older had taught him and would begin pulling his own weight, as we like to say.

The analogy is a good one, but it is not perfect with respect to what Jesus is saying. According to Jesus, the yoke he invites us to take is easy and light, the idea being that Jesus is carrying all the weight—which is absolutely true as it relates to his taking care of our sin problem. He finished that work on the cross, so it is no longer necessary (even if it were possible) to toil anymore to deal with sin. It is finished. He did it all by himself and carries all the weight in this regard. This was an amazing idea to those who had spent their entire lives carrying the burden of the expectations of God's law, along with the constant reminder from the religious elite that they weren't doing a very good job of it.

Contrast that with Jesus' further bidding to allow him to teach them what being made right with God and finding the more they were looking for really looked like. His teaching style was humble and gentle—a far cry from the arrogant and harsh hypocrisy of the Pharisees and other religious moralists. Jesus not only said that anyone could come and experience this freedom, but he also would regularly point out the fact that the legalism and self-righteousness of the religious establishment was one of the biggest obstacles to this rest he promised. He called them blind guides and said that they "crush people with impossible religious demands and never lift a finger to ease the burden" (Matthew 23:4). Jesus was declaring that those days were over. "Come to me," he said, and "I will give you rest."

What It Means to Follow

Beyond the invitation Jesus offers to all of us to come, there is the subsequent action of following. Remember what he said to the fishermen: "Come, follow me." There are a number of implications here regarding what it means to follow Jesus. First of all, it always involves a parting, or a leaving. I like to say it's the "leaving" in "believing." You know, that's what James and John said to their father when they left him in the boat: "Hey Dad, we gotta 'be-leaving' now." Okay, that was bad. But my point is still valid. Following Jesus always involves leaving something else behind.

Let me also say that I don't think this passage teaches that in order to respond to Jesus' invitation to follow, you have to up and quit your job. I would highly recommend not doing that just now. It could, for some, mean exactly that, but there's a more general principle in play here. What Jesus is asking us to walk away from is our former perspective regarding who is in control of our lives. Are we calling the shots, or are we going to allow God to do that from now on? And I don't think God calls everyone into vocational ministry, although I do think that every follower of Jesus is doing full-time ministry. We'll talk more about that in a later chapter. Jesus is, in fact, inviting them to follow him into a whole new kingdom with a brand-new King. And as his subjects, or followers, we will discover what the agenda of his kingdom looks like. He is excited about showing us the ropes and enlarging our vision for what our lives were created for. We were created for God and his kingdom. We were created not just to fish, but also to fish for men.

Maybe you also noticed in the calling of these fishermen that Jesus is calling them not just to follow him and be his disciples but also to make more disciples. On their very first encounter with Jesus, and in response to his call to be disciples, they already know that to follow Jesus also means to make disciples. After all, that's what he reiterates three years later when he instructs them to make disciples as they're going along in the world. Following Jesus includes making more disciples who follow Jesus.

On a contemporary note of application, each of us might find ourselves living like everyone else. You know, going to school, getting a good job (with hope, one we like), raising a family, and perhaps even volunteering our time and trying to make a difference in the world. Very wholesome—very safe. But instead of seeing all that as the means and possibly even the end, Jesus invites us to surrender ourselves and our plans to something better—a life in which God's plans become my plans and God promises to provide for my needs so that I don't have to worry about such things. I can truly rest in his provision. Moreover, if I'm not about pursuing my own agenda and I'm trusting God for what I need, I am in a far better position than I would be otherwise to pursue the work of his kingdom in a way that both fulfills his purposes and satisfies me. I believe this is what Jesus is talking about in Matthew 6:31–33 when he says, "So don't worry about these things saying, 'What will we eat? What will we drink? What will we wear?' These things dominate the thoughts of unbelievers, but your heavenly Father already knows your needs. Seek the kingdom of God above all else, and live righteously, and he will give you everything you need."

In other words, you may fish for a living, but now your primary identity is being a child of God and a follower of Christ. You may be a schoolteacher, but now you life's mission is teaching others how they can find the more they're looking for in Jesus. You may be a truck driver, but now what drives you is your relationship with Jesus and a commitment to living life the way he did. You may be a business manager, but now you're in the business of managing your life according to the principles of God's word and finding your place in the mission of sharing the good news of Jesus with others—and helping them to follow him too.

An invitation to follow Jesus is the invitation to finally discover what life is all about—and to become the person God has always intended for you to become. We get to trade in going to work for finding our purpose. We get to replace earning a paycheck for making an impact. We get to exchange just going through life for a life that's going somewhere—as long as the somewhere we're going is where Jesus is going. And to do that you have to follow him. That's why those fishermen left in such a hurry.

Not Everyone Chooses to Follow

While it's true that most of us will keep our jobs and still be able to follow Jesus in the spirit and intent of his calling, there are other obstacles that can keep us from following. And it has more to do with our hearts than our behavior. The thing that appeals to me so much about the way Jesus invites us to follow him is that he doesn't say that we have to do anything in order to follow him except, well, follow. He doesn't say we need to clean up our act or start going to church or try to be a better person. That's because we don't know how to do these things anyway, and he wants to show us that himself. But because Jesus knows our heart even better than we do, he sometimes throws in a caveat to our following that is specific to the individual. There's such a story in Mark chapter ten:

> As Jesus was starting out on his way to Jerusalem, a man came running up to him, knelt down, and asked, "Good Teacher, what must I do to inherit eternal life?" "Why do you call me good?" Jesus asked, "Only God is truly good. But to answer your question, you know the commandments: You must not murder. You must not commit adultery. You must not steal. You must not testify falsely. You must not cheat anyone. Honor your father and mother." "Teacher," the man replied, "I've obeyed all these commandments since I was young." Looking at the man, Jesus felt genuine love for him. "There is still one thing you haven't done," he told him. "Go and sell all your possessions and give the money to the poor, and you will have treasure in heaven. Then come, follow me." (Mark 1:17–21)

You may know this as the story of the rich young ruler. His response to Jesus is disappointing at the least. The passage goes on to say that the man's face fell (no, not literally; his countenance fell) and that he walked away very sad, "for he had many possessions" (v. 22). It may be more accurate to say that his many possessions had him. Keep in mind that Jesus had a great love for this guy and knew he was looking for more. After all, he was rich and influential already—and apparently was very religious. But he was still looking for more. As with our fishermen friends, Jesus was the more this guy was looking for. But this guy couldn't see it. Something else was in the way. Something, or should I say many things, blinded him to what it was that would finally fulfill him completely—Jesus.

This is another passage that can be misapplied if we're not careful. I don't believe that everyone who chooses to follow Jesus needs to sell everything and give it to the poor any more than everyone needs to quit his or her job. But as we've said, in order to follow Jesus, you do have to drop what you're doing—or, more accurately, what you're holding on to—if you're going to follow him for real. It just so happened that in the case of the rich young ruler, he was holding on to wealth and possessions. He didn't have them. They had him.

Notice that Jesus doesn't go running after him to restate the qualifications or try to convince him he's making a grave mistake. He lets him walk, which is exactly what Jesus does with all of us when he invites us to follow him. He's saying that the invitation is open to anyone. He's saying that he himself is the more we've all been looking for. He's saying that he's willing to teach us and show us everything, and that we can rest in his grace, both for the forgiveness of sin and the power for living. What he's not saying is that you can follow him and still hold on to something you value more than him, whatever or whoever that may be.

That's the prerequisite to following Jesus. It's nothing you have to do or become. It's something you have to let go of. The apostle Paul talked about it as throwing off old clothes in order to put new ones on. How ridiculous is the notion of putting brand-new, fresh-smelling clothes over the top of dirty, smelly ones. You cannot follow unless you leave something behind. Remember, it's the "leaving" in "believing."

Recently I noticed an interesting contrast that follows the story of the rich young ruler in Mark chapter ten. A little further on in the passage, Jesus encounters another fellow:

> Then they reached Jericho, and as Jesus and his disciples left town, a large crowd followed him. A blind beggar named Bartimaeus (son of Timaeus) was sitting beside the road. When Bartimaeus heard that Jesus of Nazareth was nearby, he began to shout, "Jesus, Son of David, have

> mercy on me!" "Be quiet!" many of the people yelled at him. But he only shouted louder, "Son of David, have mercy on me!" When Jesus heard him, he stopped and said, "Tell him to come here." So they called the blind man. "Cheer up," they said. "Come, he's calling you!" Bartimaeus threw aside his coat, jumped up, and came to Jesus. "What do you want me to do for you?" Jesus asked. "My rabbi," the blind man said, "I want to see!" And Jesus said to him, "Go, for your faith has healed you." Instantly the man could see, and he followed Jesus down the road. (Mark 10:46–52)

Notice the difference in this episode. First of all, there's a huge contrast between the socioeconomic realities of blind Bart and the rich young ruler. Again Jesus illustrates how those poor of spirit—and other things—readily see their need for God, while others of more self-sufficient means have a hard time surrendering. Secondly, the blind man refers to Jesus with an unmistakable messianic term. Anyone hearing this man's cries would have recognized the title "Son of David" as a name for the Messiah. This guy may have been physically blind, but he had extraordinary spiritual vision. He could see in Jesus what the rich man with full sight could not—and did not—see.

One last observation. The text says that Bartimaeus threw off his coat and came to Jesus. This would have been a careless decision on anyone's part, for a coat was a most valuable possession, and in the case of this poor, blind beggar, it's safe to say it was his only worldly possession. And what does he do? He abandons it to come to Jesus. He is willing to let go of everything he has in the world to go to Jesus, the Son of David, the Messiah—unlike his rich counterpart a few verses earlier. Jesus counts this as faith even before the blind man gets what he hopes Jesus will give him.

This is the part of the story that always amazes me. When Bartimaeus gets to Jesus, Jesus asks him what he wants him to do for him. Isn't it obvious? The man is blind. He wants to see! And that is exactly how he responds to Jesus' rather curious question. "Yes," he says, "I want to see." And so Jesus heals him, giving him back his physical sight, and tells him that his faith has healed him. But the truth is that he had been healed of a far more serious sight condition even before Jesus healed his eyes. He saw what Jesus was all about—that he was the Messiah, the one sent by God to deliver his people and bring them hope. It was this revelation that allowed Bartimaeus to leave everything behind (coat included) to follow Jesus.

Interestingly, Jesus doesn't invite him to follow him but rather tells him to go. But he doesn't go. As in the case of the four fishermen, he immediately follows Jesus down the road. So the rich young ruler is invited to follow and instead goes away, while blind Bartimaeus is told to go and instead follows. And it's all because of recognizing Jesus for who he is.

The "Me" in "Follow Me"

Everyone follows. Everyone follows something or someone. That can be a good thing, or that can be not so good. It's not a question as to whether we follow something or not. The question is what or whom we follow. An even more important implication is this: where is the person or thing you're following leading you to? Not only are we all following, but we're all being led somewhere as well. Have you considered that lately?

The problem is that there are so many options for following. There's religion and there's no religion. There's humanism and relativism and materialism and existentialism and moralism and fill-in-the-blank-ism. We can pursue the American dream or financial independence or relational happiness or vocational success. We deem these as our rights, no less. Not only are there myriad things to follow, but God has also given us a free will so that we can choose what it is we will follow.

You may say, "I don't follow anything; I do my own thing." Then you're following yourself, which God, of course, will let you do. But it's the same tragic error that brought sin into the world in the first place. Simply put, to follow anything other than God is idolatry—and the chief idol for all of us is self. Which is why Jesus says something about that too, in the context of following him: "Then Jesus said to his disciples, 'If any of you want to be my follower, you must turn from your selfish ways, take up your cross, and follow me. If you try to hang on to your life, you will lose it. But if you give up your life for my sake, you will save it. And what do you benefit if you gain the whole world but lose your own soul?'" (Matthew 16:24–26).

Inherent in all the invitations to follow that we've examined is the idea that we are called to die to ourselves. We might find this a strange and impossible demand if it weren't for the fact that Jesus has shown us how to do this and given us the power to do it as well, as long as we're connected, or yoked, to him. It is vital to understand now, as disciples have since the first century, that Jesus is not calling them to start a new religion or to simply ante up for a worthy cause, but to come to him. We must recognize—as blind Bartimaeus did, as the two travelers on the Road to Emmaus did, and as the original twelve he called did (though it took some time and some miracles)—that Jesus wasn't just another rabbi, albeit one who spoke to the common man, or even merely a prophet of Old Testament proportions, but that he was, in fact, the Son of God. The Messiah who was promised indeed came, but not as a deliverer from political oppression or even religious hypocrisy; rather, he came as one who could deliver us from ourselves. Of all the things we leave behind to follow Jesus, they can all be summed up in the denial of self.

So Long, Self

Dallas Willard says in his book *Renovation of the Heart* that "In the clear and forceful vision of Jesus and his kingdom, as our personality becomes progressively more reorganized around God and his eternal life, self-denial moves beyond more or less frequent acts to settled disposition and character" (p. 71). In other words, it doesn't just become a way of life; it becomes who we are. We are the church. We are his witnesses. We are followers of Christ.

It should seem obvious that denying self does not come naturally to us. We are by nature (and that being human) self-preservational. One would be seen as peculiar, if not insane, to take on the perspective of giving up his or her life in order to find it. But this is precisely what Jesus is saying we need to do in order to find true fulfillment—abundant life, as he calls it—and he means it for both here and now as well as forever. It is the capitulation to the philosophy that I am not the center of my world, but God is. God doesn't exist for me, but I exist for him. My love for God is based on who he is and not on what he can do for me. But he, in fact, has done a great deal for us—specifically, upon the cross.

Take Up Your Cross

In the days of Jesus, crosses meant one thing—death. The Roman capital punishment of crucifixion was a brutal and efficient practice. So horrific was it, in fact, that it was reserved for the vilest of criminals and treasonous enemies of the state. Vile Jesus was not. But a revolutionary—someone who was claiming a higher authority than Caesar—a king upon the throne of a superior kingdom? Oh yes. Since we have covered the efficacy of the cross of Christ pertaining to our own forgiveness in an earlier chapter, let me just say here that Jesus' obedience to the cross also served as a poignant illustration as to what it meant to live life the way he did—or, as we've been saying, to follow him.

Jesus lived his entire earthly life as a sacrifice for others. The incarnation itself (God becoming flesh) has to be seen as a sacrifice; wouldn't you agree? But even as his three-year earthly ministry begins and he's going about teaching the truth about God and his kingdom as no one ever has, he is constantly taking the backseat to others. He is always putting other peoples' needs above his own and testing the limits of his human endurance to help others discover and embrace the more they're looking for. But nothing would compare to the ultimate sacrifice he would face on the cross—or, as we call it, the passion of the Christ.

In this finale of a life of service and sacrifice, Jesus would not only accomplish the payment for the sin of the world, but he would also illustrate how the life we give up to serve others will also culminate in a resurrection not unlike the one he would experience himself. And the crucifixion and resurrection is the key to understanding that when we take up our cross and die to self in order to follow him, we too shall experience new and eternal life. Jesus' constant reminders to his disciples of how they ought to serve one another as he served them would be highlighted in this final, incredible act of love.

Jesus once used the occasion of a debate among the disciples as to who would have dibs on seats next to Jesus in heaven to remind them of the counterintuitive nature of his kingdom: "But Jesus called them together and said, 'You know that rulers in this world lord it over their people, and officials flaunt their authority over those under them. But among you it will be different. Whoever wants to be a leader among you must be your servant, and whoever wants to be first among you must become your slave. For even the Son of Man came not to be served but to serve others and to give his life as a ransom for many'" (Matthew 20:25–28).

So Jesus has just told his disciples that he's going to Jerusalem to die, and all they can think about is what position they'll be getting in his kingdom. Unbelievably, they don't respond or even seem to react to what Jesus has just said about his impending death. It seems it's getting late in the discipleship course and these guys still don't get it! But they soon will.

Following Leads to Becoming

So what happens when people really do deny themselves, take up their cross, and follow Jesus? Well, pretty much the same thing people do when they submit themselves to become the apprentice of someone who has mastered a trade, a sport, or an art. They become like that person. This is the simplest definition that I can fathom of what it means to be spiritually mature: to be like Jesus.

And if Christlikeness is the metric of spiritual formation, then it is fair to say that everything falls under this descriptor. Thus, to be the church is to be like Jesus. To be a witness is to be like Jesus. To be a follower of Christ is to be like Jesus.

To be a Christian is to be like Jesus.

And what does that look like?

It looks a lot like love.

CHAPTER 7

IT LOOKS A LOT LIKE LOVE

> But when the Pharisees heard that he had silenced the Sadducees with his reply, they met together to question him again. One of them, an expert in religious law, tried to trap him with this question: "Teacher, which is the most important commandment in the law of Moses?" Jesus replied, "You must love the LORD your God with all your heart, all your soul, and all your mind. This is the first and greatest commandment. A second is equally important: Love your neighbor as yourself. The entire law and all the demands of the prophets are based on these two commandments."
>
> —Matthew 22:34–40

I remember from years ago, when I was a young boy, a television commercial about a guy who is running busily through an airport and bumps into a small boy who is putting together a puzzle. My mind recalls this in black-and-white—yikes! But we won't get into that now. Anyway, the guy's briefcase sideswipes the child, and puzzle pieces go airborne. Feeling the tension between missing his flight and helping this kid, the man glances back and forth between his watch and this pitiful array of puzzle and child. Finally, he gives a subtle sigh that blends into a half smile and sets down his luggage to help pick up the pieces. The last camera angle of the scene is from above, looking down at the little boy as he thoughtfully asks the man kneeling beside him, "Mister, are you God?"

When is the last time you had someone mistake you for God? I know that's kind of ridiculous. Some people may think they're God. When we live totally for ourselves, we try to play God. But when we place the needs of others above our own, even in small acts of love and kindness, we look a little bit like God. Why? Because God looks a lot like love.

I'd like to suggest in this chapter that the clearest example of what it means to be the church rather than going to church—and what it means to be a witness instead of going witnessing—has mostly to do with love. Being the church looks a lot like love. Being a witness looks a lot like love. Following Jesus and becoming like Jesus—well, I think you know it looks a lot like love. As is the case with any successful apprentice, your desire is to take on the character, skills, knowledge, and attitude of the master you're being apprenticed by. And if our Master, Jesus Christ, lived a life primarily characterized by love for and service to others, so, then, should we.

Among the many debates and trick questions that the religious hierarchy pitted Jesus against, none is more significant than the exchange he has in this chapter's epigraph. In hopes of creating confusion and competition among the known law of God found in the Ten Commandments, the Pharisees ask Jesus to apply a rating system. Jesus knows their evil hearts, yet instead of his characteristic reply with another question, he responds quickly and confidently by saying, "You must love the LORD your God with all your heart, all your soul, and all your mind. This is the first and greatest commandment. A second is equally important: 'Love your neighbor as yourself.'"

The Great Commandment

Oh, Jesus is good. His answer at first doesn't sound anything like what we recognize as the Ten Commandments—you know, "thou shalt . . ." and "thou shalt not . . ." But in fact he covers all ten with what would have been a very familiar phrase from the book of Deuteronomy. "Loving the Lord with all your heart, soul, mind, and strength" was what the Hebrews referred to as the Shema, which is the verb for "listen up." You can see that more clearly in its context: "Listen, O Israel! The LORD is our God, the LORD alone. And you must love the LORD your God with all your heart, all your soul, and all your strength. And you must commit yourselves wholeheartedly to these commands that I am giving you today" (Deuteronomy 6:4–6).

Jesus is simply stating that the commandments (all of them) can be summed up with loving God first, and with your whole being. His detractors, of course, would not have any argument with his distillation of the law to loving God first and foremost. But what may have caused one or two to scratch their heads is his placement of of loving your neighbor on equal footing with loving God. And if you take a closer look at the Ten Commandments, you can see the reason for this.

Commandments one through four have to do with loving God (i.e., having no other gods before him, making no graven images or idols, not misrepresenting his name, and honoring the Sabbath). Commandments five through ten then focus on loving others (i.e., honoring your parents, not murdering, not committing adultery, not stealing, not lying, and not coveting the possessions of others). It makes sense that if you really loved other people, you wouldn't do any of these things against them. And as Jesus seems to suggest, in his ordering of the reply, a complete love for God is the catalyst and source for being able to love others. We now know this pair of commands as the Great Commandment.

I love how Dallas Willard says this in his book *Renovation of the Heart*: "Only love of God frames and supports love of neighbor, giving it right direction and the power to carry out its aim of goodness within the kingdom. And love of God and neighbor gradually pulls the entire structure of the person into proper alignment" (pp. 70–71). In other words, if your life is in proper alignment with God and you're becoming more like Jesus, it looks a lot like love. And Jesus says this is the one legitimate way to tell if a person loves God—or not.

The Litmus of Love

So inextricably tied are the notions of loving God and loving one's neighbor that as this thought pervaded the early church's teaching, and that of the apostle Paul, it got yet another abbreviation. Paul does this twice in his writings. He does so first in Galatians 5:14: "For the whole law can be summed up in this one command: 'Love your neighbor as yourself.'" And he does so again in Romans 13:8–10: "Owe nothing to anyone—except for your obligation to love one another. If you love your neighbor, you will fulfill the requirements of God's law. For the commandments say, 'You must not commit adultery. You must not murder. You must not steal. You must not covet.' These—and other such commandments—are summed up in this one commandment: 'Love your neighbor as yourself.' Love does no wrong to others, so love fulfills the requirements of God's law."

I remember the first time I recognized this in these two Pauline passages. I reckoned that Paul could not have been committing the huge oversight that seemed to be. How could he not put "loving God first" prior to "loving one's neighbor"? But my suspicions were laid to rest when I realized that the idea of "loving God first" was a *given* for Paul. Knowing that the only way we can love our neighbor is predicated by our love for God, Paul simply states the obvious. Those who love God with all their heart will inevitably be people who also love their neighbors.

It is the litmus of love.

This truth is also supported in inarguable terms in the later writings of John: "Dear friends, let us continue to love one another, for love comes from God. Anyone who loves is a child of God and knows God. But anyone who does not love does not know God, for God is love" (1 John 4:7–8). Thus, being related to God as his child implies a spiritual DNA that reflects the characters and qualities of God—love by far being the most prominent of those qualities. This doesn't assume that everyone who is kind to another has this relationship with God. But the consistent and ever-increasing love for others (which for Jesus would go on to extend to our enemies as well) is a valid sign of being born of his Spirit.

The Good Samaritan

In the gospel of Luke's version of the Great Commandment, there's an interesting follow-up question to his reply. It would be best to view it in its entirety:

> One day an expert in religious law stood up to test Jesus by asking him this question: "Teacher, what should I do to inherit eternal life?" Jesus replied, "What does the law of Moses say? How do you read it?" The man answered, "You must love the Lord your God with all your heart, all your soul, all your strength, and all your mind." And, "Love your neighbor as yourself." "Right!" Jesus told him. "Do this and you will live!" The man wanted to justify his actions, so he asked Jesus, "And who is my neighbor?" Jesus replied with a story: "A Jewish man was traveling on a trip from Jerusalem to Jericho, and he was attacked by bandits. They stripped him of his clothes, beat him up, and left him half dead beside the road. By chance a priest came along. But when he saw the man lying there, he crossed to the other side of the road and passed him by. A Temple assistant walked over and looked at him lying there, but he also passed by on the other side. Then a despised Samaritan came along, and when he saw the man, he felt compassion for him. Going over to him, the Samaritan soothed his wounds with olive oil and wine and bandaged them. Then he put the man on his own donkey and took him to an inn, where he took care of him. The next day he handed the innkeeper two silver coins, telling him, 'Take care of this man. If his bill runs higher than this, I'll pay you the next time I'm here.' Now which of these three would you say was a neighbor to the man who was attacked by bandits?" Jesus asked. The man replied, "The one who showed him mercy." Then Jesus said, "Yes, now go and do the same." (Luke 10:25–37)

Okay, so this guy answers correctly to the litmus of love idea and the Great Commandment. But for further justification of his own righteousness, he wants some clarification on who exactly qualifies as a neighbor. After all, let's be clear; I'm not sure he liked Jesus' answer.

I find the story of the Good Samaritan to be a fascinating one. I suppose Jesus' audience would have found it more provocative. First of all, he uses a racially despised Samaritan as the hero in the story, in contrast to the villains, who both happen to be among the religious elite. The priest and the Levite pass by the wounded man on the road, apparently too busy doing "God's work" or fearing the stigma of being ceremonially unclean for coming near to or touching a dead body. But in the story as Jesus tells it, he is not dead, but only "mostly dead." (Okay, I couldn't help using the line from *The Princess Bride*). Now that I ponder it, the religious leaders in the crowd probably found it to be more than provocative. They were most likely furious. As Jesus often did, he was telling the story against them.

But for the more general audience, there are some wonderful lessons on what real love looks like. As you follow the story, I think you'll recognize three distinct layers of love. One might title this message "The Way of Loving."

1. Along-the-Way Loving

All three of the travelers along this road of misfortune were simply going about their normal day's routine. They were heading somewhere for some planned purpose when they happened upon this beaten and bloodied man. But it is only the Samaritan who takes the time to investigate the situation. He certainly had other things to do; he might even be late for his flight. (Remember the commercial at the opening of this chapter?) Yet he allows his plans to be interrupted by what he considers to be a matter of greater importance. Meanwhile, the preachers simply walk on by.

This along-the-way loving is one of the characteristics of someone who *is* the church rather than someone who *goes* to church. The idea is that loving God and loving others is a 24-7-365 proposition. And the real impact of being the church takes place in regular places and common situations. The opportunities that we have to be the salt and light of Jesus in this world are of the everyday variety. We just need to be aware. We need to take regular looks around to simply see who's in our path. And if there's someone near us who has a need, that becomes the priority, regardless of what my planner says. In fact, that's the way I think Jesus defines "neighbor" for this guy who is asking the question: A neighbor is anyone who is near you and has a need. And so we have opportunities every day of our lives to love along the way.

2. In-the-Way Loving

Now the Samaritan traveler takes a step beyond loving along the way. What he does next can be described as loving someone who is in the way. He assesses the painful damage done here and proceeds to provide medical assistance for this poor man. He cleanses and bandages his wounds and places him upon the donkey he had been perched upon himself just moments before. The broken man's caregiver would now travel by foot. Keep in mind that this is a Samaritan, who by rights you would expect to show the same kind of discrimination for this Jewish victim as the Jews would have for him. But he lovingly lifts this man upon his donkey and heads for some hospice. Maybe that's why they call him good.

Stop and think for a moment about the things that get in our way on a daily basis. I, for one, confess that interruptions in my plans and delays in my schedule are pet peeves of mine. I'm growing in this area of my spiritual formation, but how many times have we actually acted more like the priest and the Levite than the Good Samaritan? These days I'm learning to slow down and look around. I think that's a good mantra for a lot of us. Just s—l—o—w down and look around. We always come across people along the way in our daily life. A few of those people have needs that identify them as being in the way. Jesus calls them our neighbors, and he said we need to love on them.

3. Out-of-the-Way Loving

If the story of the Good Samaritan ended here, it would be a good story—one of compassion and goodwill. But this story has one more layer, and it's the place where love stands out as being something that goes beyond simply doing the right thing. It's about going out of your way to love.

The Samaritan (who already has done enough to earn the descriptor "good") arrives at the next town, where he provides convalescence for his wounded passenger. He gives the owner of the establishment a cash advance and asks him to care for the man until he returns. When he comes back, he will pay him for any additional expenses the original payment didn't cover. He assures the new caregiver that he will take care of everything so that his patient is left in good hands. And then he sets off for the appointment that started him on his journey that morning.

Are you kidding me? This is incredible love. Even if it were Jew-to-Jew or Samaritan-to-Samaritan, it would be an amazing act of kindness. But for a Samaritan to show this kind of love and compassion to a Jew was unheard of. It was not humanly conceivable. It was thought of as ungodly! I think we're tempted many times to do what we feel is necessary when it comes to loving our neighbor. We tend to weigh factors like convenience and personal sacrifice, and if we're really honest, maybe we conside what kind of return or benefit may be in play. I know how horrible that sounds, but we're all capable of it.

But the Good Samaritan places this social and cultural enemy's needs above his own and loves him. He loves him along the way. He loves him in the way. And he loves him out of the way. And never once do we get the impression that he has any agenda other than love. In fact, if there's an agenda, you can't really call it love. Love has no agenda. Love is the agenda. In other words, the kind of love that erupts out of our love for God as we fulfill our role in being the church, being witnesses, and following Jesus is a selfless, sacrificial love without any strings attached.

This is the evidence (or the litmus test) that the Holy Spirit is living in us and that we are allowing him to live out of us as well. How conscious are you in your day-to-day living about the people you see along the way? And what if those people present the kind of obvious needs that you cannot avoid, causing them to be in the way? Are you willing to embrace the interruption as an opportunity to love, or will you walk on by to tend to your own agenda? And most significant of all, are you willing to pay the price for extravagant care by going well out of your way to love? Because loving people along, in, and out of the way is what Jesus said it looked like to love your neighbor. Jesus and the apostle Paul would also teach regarding this litmus of love. They referred to it as the fruit of God's Spirit.

You Know a Tree by Its Fruit

When I was in high school, I participated in a vocational cabinetmaking class in which as part of our studies we learned how to identify different species of trees. Mostly we looked at the shapes of leaves or the textures of bark, but in some cases the tree bore a nut or a fruit that easily gave that tree its name. I enjoyed being able to pick out the more obscure and less popular species, but there's nothing like having the hard-core evidence of an apple hanging from a limb. Apple trees bear apples, of course. But you knew that already.

Jesus knew people knew such things as well when he used the same example to talk about life in his kingdom. For example: "A good tree produces good fruit, and a bad tree produces bad fruit. A good tree can't produce bad fruit, and a bad tree can't produce good fruit. So every tree that does not produce good fruit is chopped down and thrown into the fire. Yes, just as you can identify a tree by its fruit, so you can identify people by their actions" (Matthew 7:17–20).

We can label ourselves with any name we want—even call ourselves Christians—but our actions will always tell the true story. The gospel of Jesus isn't just about Jesus; it *is* Jesus. And yes, we must believe in his death on the cross for our forgiveness and to be born of his Spirit and resurrection to life. But we also must allow his Spirit to flow out of us in order to reflect his character and image. And as I've mentioned before, it looks a lot like love. Love is the fruit of the Spirit. I'll get to more on this in a moment, but I want to carry on with this thought of being connected to Jesus.

Divine and De Branches

In John chapter 15:1–8 Jesus uses another fruit metaphor to describe the kingdom of God:

> I am the true grapevine, and my Father is the gardener. He cuts off every branch of mine that doesn't produce fruit, and he prunes the branches that do bear fruit so they will produce even more. You have already been pruned and purified by the message I have given you. Remain in me, and I will remain in you. For a branch cannot produce fruit if it is severed from the vine, and you cannot be fruitful unless you remain in me.

> Yes, I am the vine; you are the branches. Those who remain in me, and I in them, will produce much fruit. For apart from me you can do nothing. Anyone who does not remain in me is thrown away like a useless branch and withers. Such branches are gathered into a pile to be burned. But if you remain in me and my words remain in you, you may ask for anything you want, and it will be granted! When you produce much fruit, you are my true disciples. This brings great glory to my Father.

In the above passage, which may be familiar to many, Jesus makes it abundantly clear that the fruit his followers will bear and the life his disciples will lead will only be possible as long as they are connected to him in the way that a branch is connected to a vine or a root.

It's pretty simple, really. The root is the source of nourishment for the entire plant and is basically hidden from view. The rest of the plant's extension through other branches carries the nutrition all the way out to the end, where the leaves, buds, and fruit are produced. The branches are very much a part of the tree (or the kingdom, the body, or the church), but for the most part they contribute to the health of the structure by allowing the real source of life coming from the root to pass through them. The branches provide a vehicle, or a conduit, from the root to the fruit.

That's why branches that aren't connected are incapable of producing fruit. It reminds me of something I saw one autumn afternoon as I was driving home from my office. The hardwood trees along the way through our neighborhood were brilliant with reds, yellows, and oranges—I mean the color orange. Oh, you know what I mean; I live in Pennsylvania! Anyway, I happened to notice this rather large limb hanging down from a particularly beautiful maple tree (remember, I know my trees), which appeared to have broken off back at the trunk and was hanging on by a few fibers. Alas, its leaves were not brilliant, but brown and dry and withered. It looked like an outcast among its colorful colleagues. I remember thinking, *That's what Jesus was talking about.* Apart from him, I cannot live the colorful life of love and selflessness that reflects his image. And Jesus doesn't say it's difficult to produce fruit when disconnected from him; he says it's impossible!

So in reality, a branch like you or me doesn't produce the fruit of the Spirit; it simply stays close and connected to the Vine—which, of course, is Jesus. He's the Vine, and we're the branches. It's our continual surrender to Jesus as we follow him and our submission to his Spirit's direction and desire in our lives that allows us to bear much fruit. As the writer of Hebrews rightly mandates, "Let us fix our eyes on Jesus, the author and perfecter of our faith" (12:2). Our devotion and attention are given to Jesus, allowing his Spirit to flow through us, and then fruit . . . happens. It's that fundamental choice to yield to Jesus that brings us to our final thoughts on love as the fruit of God's Spirit.

The Fruit of the Spirit

Though there are numerous forms of this list, arranged in various places and contexts in the New Testament, none is more familiar and quoted than Galatians 5:22–23: "But the Holy Spirit produces this kind of fruit in our lives: love, joy, peace, patience, kindness, goodness, faithfulness, gentleness, and self-control. There is no law against these things!"

Anyone who grew up in a Sunday school environment sang or recited these nine classic virtues of the Christian life. Here the apostle Paul gives us some finer detail on what it looks like to love. Because even if you agree that following Jesus, being a witness of Christ, or being the church looks a lot like love, it begs the question, what does this love look like?

Well, it looks like bringing joy into someone's discouragement. It looks like working for peace in a broken relationship. It looks like being patient when someone in need is in the middle of the road on a very busy day. It looks like being kind when everything inside you wants to lash out. It looks like doing the right thing when no one is looking. It looks like remaining faithful when the challenges of a commitment require that you do the heavy lifting. It looks like being gentle when rougher tactics would be more convenient and perhaps somewhat effective. It looks like choosing to do the loving thing. It's always a choice, and that's what Paul means by "self-control."

I noticed at one point in the past that this list of the fruit of the Spirit seems to be more unified than at first glance. What I mean is that it's not like you can choose to be patient but not choose to be faithful. It's not a buffet; it's a fruit salad—and there's no picking out just the items you like. Another aspect of this holistic perspective is that all of the virtues listed between the first one (love) and the last one (self-control) are, in fact, various expressions that refer to choosing to do the loving thing.

Encouraging someone is the loving thing to do. Being patient with someone is an act of love. Remaining faithful to a spouse or a friend in difficult times is the willful decision to love. I don't know about you, but it seems obvious to me. What I have deduced is that love and self-control form a set of bookends for everything between them, as pictured below:

LOVE SELF-CONTROL
joy peace patience kindness goodness faithfulness gentleness

Therefore, the person who submits to the inclinations of the Holy Spirit is exercising self-control, or what we might call spiritual control. This would, of course, lead us to loving and serving others, but it also leads us to resist the temptation to act in ways contrary to God's character and desire. Of course I'm talking about all the kinds of behaviors we would consider to be ungodly. Prior to the verses enumerating the fruit of the Spirit, Paul says, "So I say, let the Holy Spirit guide your lives. Then you won't be doing what your sinful nature craves. The sinful nature wants to do evil, which is just the opposite of what the Spirit wants. And the Spirit gives us desires that are the opposite of what the sinful nature desires. These two forces are constantly fighting each other, so you are not free to carry out your good intentions. But when you are directed by the Spirit, you are not under obligation to the law of Moses" (Galatians 5:16–18).

In the same way Jesus says that producing fruit is impossible apart from him, Paul is also saying that apart from allowing the Holy Spirit to have control, living a Christlike life is impossible. What's more, he even suggests in both of these places we've examined in Galatians 5 that it has nothing to do with obeying the law of God. And it's a curious statement he makes at the end of the list in verse twenty-three. He says, if you'll remember, "There is no law against these things."

Well of course there's no law against these things. Why would there be? Does that statement seem as strange to you as it does to me? But I think there is a sensible understanding of this. Paul is essentially saying that there is no law on the books that could ever make anyone live up to these virtues consistently and sincerely. There's something missing in the heart of a person that a law could never produce. What is even further implied is that the law of God (or the law of Moses, as he refers to it) doesn't help us to do that either. Is he honestly suggesting that the Ten Commandments, which Jesus distills into "love God and love your neighbor," have no power to help us actually love God and our neighbor? Precisely.

God's law, or what we can consider to be God's standard and expectation, only serves to prove to us how incapable we are of living up to that standard. The law of God serves to point us to our need for something beyond ourselves—something, or more accurately someone, to help us do what we cannot do though God expects it. That someone, of course, is Jesus and the power of his Spirit living inside us. His grace is applied to our forgiveness on the cross and also to our being refined in holiness through new life in the Spirit. What the law couldn't do to perfect righteousness in us, a life surrendered and yielded to Jesus can. You can read Paul's further discussion on this in Galatians chapter three.

I Am the Church

So what would it look like if someone relied on the power of the Spirit in his or her life to follow Jesus in the way he lived his life? And what would it look like if others who were also following Jesus in this Spirit-controlled life came together to combine their gifts and passions in the mission of sharing the gospel with those who still don't comprehend the infinite love and grace of God? Yes, it would still look a lot like love. But it would also look like the church. As an individual follower of Jesus who loves God and my neighbor, I am the church; I don't go to church. And as the collective gathering of Christ-followers who use our gifts to love God and our neighbors, we are the church; we don't go to church. That's why God has given us all the gifts and abilities we have. Because we can only *be* the church in its most complete form as we *are* the church together.

And if we all are the church, then we are all ministers too!

CHAPTER 8

WE'RE ALL IN FULL-TIME MINISTRY

> And you are living stones that God is building into his spiritual temple.
> What's more you are his holy priests. Through the mediation of Jesus Christ, you offer spiritual sacrifices that please God . . . for you are a chosen people.
> You are royal priests, a holy nation, God's very own possession. As a result, you can show others the goodness of God, for he called you out of the darkness and into his wonderful light.
>
> —1 Peter 2:5, 9

There's a guy in our church, Brad, who has been a part of our church family almost from the beginning of our church's existence in 1995. Brad works for the US Postal Service, delivering mail in our town—mostly by foot. He's a great guy, and everything I've ever seen him do, he has done with enthusiasm. For many years now he has invested his life in our student ministry. The kids love Brad, and Brad loves them. He's hard not to like, with his energy and humor. And he has another very important attribute for youth ministry—he's just a crazy guy.

Brad has also developed well as a teacher over the years and has even done some preaching at our weekend services. As a matter of fact, while I'm out of town working on this chapter, Brad will do the weekend speaking. Brad is a great example of someone who lives the gospel seven days a week. Whether it's his mail route or walking down the halls of our church building or reserving Sunday afternoon and evening strictly for his wife and two daughters, Brad is the real deal.

Recently Brad was sharing with our NexGen pastor about some thoughts he was having about going into full-time ministry. I think he's been feeling this in his heart for a long time, and he was communicating some frustration as to when and how that might happen. My response to Brad was, "Dude, you're doing full-time ministry. You have been doing full-time ministry for a long time now." I think he knew what I was saying, but I'm not sure he really believed it. I'm not sure many other Christ followers believe it either.

I already covered in some detail in chapter four the idea that in Christ we are all priests, his temple, living stones, and sacrifices. Moving beyond those positional truths, I'd like to lean into the practical aspects of what it means to *be* the church in the normative sense of our daily lives and experiences. To put it plainly, every believer is a minister—and not just a minister, but a full-time minister. In a most general way, we're all in the ministry of reconciliation, or helping people find their way back to God. But in more specific ways, we've been created for a specific ministry role that is uniquely suited to our gifts, personality, and passions. Let me begin with a more general perspective.

A Ministry of Reconciliation

1 Corinthians 5:17–21 says this about every believer:

This means that anyone who belongs to Christ has become a new person. The old life is gone; a new life has begun! And all of this is a gift from God, who brought us back to himself through Christ. And God has given us this task of reconciling people to him. For God was in Christ, reconciling the world to himself, no longer counting people's sins against them. And he gave us this wonderful message of reconciliation. So we are Christ's ambassadors; God is making his appeal through us. We speak for

Christ when we plead, "Come back to God!" For God made Christ, who never sinned, to be the offering for our sin, so that we could be made right with God through Christ.

Our primary ministry, if you will, is the ministry of reconciliation. It's the ministry of reaching people with the life-changing gospel of Jesus Christ. It's every believer's responsibility and calling to help others see the wonder and freedom of a life transformed by God. This should be every church's primary mission objective as well. But remember that we don't *go* to church; we *are* the church. And so there are certainly larger strategies for churches to reach people through their weekend experiences and outreach events, but the most effective and comprehensive method is when everyone goes home from church on the weekend to be the church throughout the week. "Go be the church!" has been our weekly dismissal slogan for some time now.

And while our church's strategy includes missional outreach and cultural relevance in the weekend services, the primary mission field is everywhere the feet of those who come to church take them as they leave. For Brad it's his mail route. For my wife it's her kindergarten class. For my young adult children it's a college context (boy, I am getting old). For one of my good friends it's being a pharmacist. For another dear friend and mentor it's operating a bed-and-breakfast—although he and his wife's real passion in life has been founding and leading a mission organization that takes hundreds of people a year to a community among the Jamaican poor. For me it's being a pastor. And each and every one of us is in full-time ministry!

When Jesus told his disciples in Acts chapter one to tell people about him everywhere, he meant *everywhere.* And they were to do that in the context of being witnesses, not in the context of going witnessing. We get the opportunity to be witnesses every day of our lives and in every setting. As noted in 1 Peter in the beginning of this chapter, we get to show people the goodness of God because we've been called out of the darkness and into his light. And if you're in the light, you join forces with others who are in the light to impact those who are still in the darkness. And bear in mind that we do this by showing them God's goodness, not by emphasizing God's wrath. It really does look a lot like love.

Salt and Light

In order for a light to have any effect on darkness, it must come into some proximity with darkness. The same thing is true of salt as well. It does nothing for bland taste unless it comes in contact with the thing that's bland. This is where Jesus is going when he introduces this idea in his Sermon on the Mount. I have already quoted this in chapter four, but I will provide it again here:

You are the salt of the earth. But what good is salt if it has lost its flavor? Can you make it salty again? It will be thrown out and trampled underfoot as worthless. You are the light of the world—like a city on a hilltop that cannot be hidden. No one lights a lamp and then puts it under a basket. Instead, a lamp is placed on a stand, where it gives light to everyone in the house. In the same way, let your good deeds shine out for all to see, so that everyone will praise your heavenly Father.

This very familiar passage on evangelism speaks of our witness being more organic and natural than some of our traditional ideas of strategic efforts in witnessing. It's more of the way our lives permeate our culture, our neighborhoods, our workplaces, our parties, our ballgames, our eateries, our service clubs, our volunteer fire companies, etc. And of particular note is the fact that it's our good deeds (or, as Peter expresses it, "the goodness of God") people see, not our specific theology or denominational affiliation. They see how good God is in how good we are to them.

The common fallacy here is that we believe our goodness or our good works make us good people. We assume that our following the rules and, as we say, being a good Christian have more to do with conduct and adherence to religious expectations than being a good person. Not that conduct is irrelevant to being a witness, for we have already discussed the matter of right behavior as a by-product of following Jesus and living a Spirit-controlled life. But people don't glorify God by observing other people behaving rightly. They glorify God by seeing other people reflecting the image and character of God in the way they love, show mercy, treat others respectfully, and forgive. In our being good to them—rather than just being good—they come out of darkness and into the light of Jesus, who is of course, the Light of the World.

After a person has "seen the light," as we like to say, the process of discipleship through apprenticing and growing in their new relationship with God take on a whole new velocity. It is here, in the context of spiritual formation and mentoring, that we can call fellow believers to higher standards of conduct and attitude—keeping in mind again that it's not something we are capable of in our own power, but only as we rely on the sustaining grace and power of the Holy Spirit. Unfortunately, a detailed discussion of this concept is beyond the scope of this book's purpose. For a more comprehensive treatment of this idea of spiritual formation, I highly recommend the book *Renovation of the Heart* by Dallas Willard.

Made for Ministry

I'd like to talk a little about the second most fulfilling aspect of following Jesus and being the church. Of course the first is finding our purpose and fulfillment as a child of God, and being restored to his family and his kingdom through the sacrifice of his Son and the gift of his Spirit. But once that new and eternal life is ours, the next most incredible reality is discovering the ministry role we were created for. The truth is, we are not just saved *from* something (namely, a life of sin without God) but we are also saved *for* something (a life of ministry and service). Nothing says it better than this passage in Ephesians 2:8–10: "God saved you by his grace when you believed. And you can't take credit for this; it is a gift from God. Salvation is not a reward for the good things we have done, so none of us can boast about it. For we are God's masterpiece. He has created us anew in Christ Jesus, so we can do the good things he planned for us long ago."

We are reminded here for good reason that there's nothing we can do to earn this wonderful salvation. We cannot achieve it by being good or by doing good works. This is where so many people get it backward. Even if they understand that they come to Christ by grace, they somehow assume that moving forward and maintaining this standing with God is based on what they do for him. But the text makes it clear that the good works that God has in mind for us to do even before we are born come out of our grace-given and Spirit-filled life—not as a means to achieve that life.

And this is no contradiction with what the New Testament writer James says in his book about faith without works being dead—or not really faith at all. James too, espouses the truth that we are saved by faith alone and yet that authentic saving faith based on God's mercy and grace will inevitably lead to a life committed to loving and serving others (i.e., good works). And at some point along the way, we will be filled with joy to discover that God has not only saved us for doing good things but also that he has created us to be good at doing good things in a specific ministry role or function.

Gifts Added to Fruit

As we already discussed in the previous chapter, what Jesus emphasized as the evidence of life in his kingdom was the fruit of the Spirit—or, in a word, love. This is to be the primary identifier (or litmus test) of a follower of Jesus. But too often in the church, we put more emphasis on the gifts of the Spirit than we do the fruit of the Spirit. So as long as someone is serving and using his or her gifts, that person is doing the will of the Lord. But it's a grave mistake to value the talented ministry gift someone is using for the work of God if his or her life doesn't also reflect his character.

For example, a pastor may have an extraordinary teaching gift but may not exercise spiritual control over a blazing temper or legendary impatience. A woman may serve faithfully in a children's ministry for years and yet portray a lack of kindness or gentleness in her demeanor. Two people could be serving beside each other on a leadership board, helping to navigate the vision and mission of the church, all the while having unsettled personal issues that afford little peace between them. Or another saint might greet people with a handshake and a smile every weekend at the doors of the church and yet never bother to wave hello to a neighbor across the lawn. It just doesn't make any sense to value the gifts of the Spirit over the fruit of the Spirit. It may seem obvious, but it is oftentimes not the practice.

Spiritual Gifts and Being the Church

Having said that—and assuming we're committed to moving on with the "fruit first" mentality—let's apply, in an acceptable way, the use of our spiritual gifts in the context of being the church. If, as I have written, church is something we are and not just something we go to, then we should realize that the use of our gifts isn't limited to the confines of traditional roles during the weekend gathering.

Someone who has the gift of teaching can just as effectively serve God's kingdom as the smoking cessation class facilitator at the local high school as he or she can leading a Bible study. A person might be just as good of a witness by volunteering at the local free clinic as in the nursery. (I can't believe I just said that. We're always in need of loving people serving in the nursery!) A craftsman who worked on the Habitat for Humanity project in his community would be just as much a follower of Jesus when he's constructing the manger and stable for the annual live nativity. A woman with mad management skills could love her neighbor just as fruitfully by helping organize a local food pantry as she could by serving on the church's leadership team. You see, if you really believe that you don't go to church but that you are the church, you will see serving opportunities at every corner and on every day of the week.

Please understand that I am not discounting all the wonderful roles and responsibilities people participate in each week when they serve on the church's ministry-specific teams. Our church thrives each and every week because of hundreds of people who volunteer their time and utilize their gifts for what happens inside our walls. But when you embed the "I am the church" philosophy into your heart and mind, ministry takes on a much more holistic and integrated flavor. You start understanding that you are the church when you're at home, at school, at work, at the Little League field, in the checkout line, and so on. And yes, you are the church when you're at church too. Although I have to say it's easier and more expected there.

A Mature Church Is a Church That Loves

In what may be the most important foundational verse in the Bible on spiritual gifts and their role in the church, the apostle Paul speaks of the equipping gifts that serve to help others discover and develop their gifts so the church can be complete and effective. It's not my purpose to hone in on the value of equipping and reproducing at this juncture; there are a host of other books that cover this territory nicely. One in particular that

I have benefited from and recommend highly is *The Equipping Church* by Sue Mallory. What I would like to spotlight, however, is what Paul points to as the outcome of a fully-equipped, gifts-operating church. See if you can pick it out in the following passage:

Now these are the gifts Christ gave to the church: the apostles, the prophets, the evangelists, and the pastors and teachers. Their responsibility is to equip God's people to do his work and build up the church, the body of Christ. This will continue until we all come to such unity in our faith and knowledge of God's Son that we will be mature in the Lord, measuring up to the full and complete standard of Christ. Then we will no longer be immature like children. We won't be tossed and blown about by every wind of new teaching. We will not be influenced when people try to trick us with lies so clever they sound like the truth. Instead, we will speak the truth in love, growing in every way more and more like Christ, who is the head of his body, the church. He makes the whole body fit together perfectly. As each part does its own special work, it helps the other parts grow, so that the whole body is healthy and growing and full of love. (Ephesians 4:11–16)

It's quite clear that leading and apprenticing and teaching truth are all very important qualities in the church that is growing in maturity. But it's the definition of "maturity" that must catch our attention. Paul speaks of "measuring up to the full and complete standard of Christ," and as each part does its own specific ministry, "the whole body is healthy and growing and full of love." Paul's description here of a healthy, mature church is one that is full of love. All of the gifts given to individuals for ministry come together for the purpose of becoming more like Jesus. The leading, the teaching, the equipping—all of these are used to cultivate a community of Christ followers who live their lives the way Jesus did. And when we who are the church, the body of Christ, follow the lead of our head (Jesus), we go on loving God and loving our neighbor every day of life and everywhere life takes us. We're all ministers, and we're all doing it full-time.

Another place where we see this idea of love as the end of the means is in 1 Timothy 1:5: "The purpose of my instruction is that all believers would be filled with love that comes from a pure heart, a clear conscience, and genuine faith. But some people have missed this whole point. They have turned away from these things and spend their time in meaningless discussions. They want to be known as teachers of the law of Moses, but they don't know what they are talking about, even though they speak so confidently."

It's a profound thing for Paul (who wrote two-thirds of the New Testament) to say the purpose of all of his teaching was to make believers be full of love. He goes on to make that point that those who think Christianity is just about going to church or being a good person are still missing the point. A lot of people today are still missing the same point.

Unfortunately, churches and individuals who miss or ignore this vital truth end up in the same foul mess the Pharisees and religious leaders were mired in during the time of Jesus. With their legalism and judgment they had erected huge walls between the masses and God. Those walls represented the impossible prerequisites that the religious structure demanded of people, and in their arrogance and hypocrisy, they manipulated the people by pretending to have achieved righteousness for themselves. There were walls of guilt and walls of prejudice and walls of exclusion. Jesus would come to tear down those walls. He said he would build his church. We would build it with him.

And it would be a church without walls.

CHAPTER 9

A CHURCH WITHOUT WALLS

> We have an altar from which the priests in the Tabernacle have no right to eat. Under the old system, the high priest brought the blood of animals into the Holy Place as a sacrifice for sin, and the bodies of the animals were burned outside the camp. So also Jesus suffered and died outside the city gates to make his people holy by means of his own blood. So let us go out to him, outside the camp, and bear the disgrace he bore. For this world is not our permanent home; we are looking forward to a home yet to come.
>
> —Hebrews 13:10–14

The lady ahead of me in the checkout line kept looking at the words printed on the front of my T-shirt. I could tell by her countenance and body language she wasn't very pleased. Oh, it wasn't anything profane or offensive—at least I didn't think so—but something told me she wanted to share her opinion. So I initiated the conversation.

"You probably wonder what this means," I said to her, "the words on my shirt, that is?"

"Yes," she said. "Why don't you go to church?"

Yes, printed in bright yellow letters on the purple T-shirt I was wearing that day was the phrase "I don't go to church." I think she was a little offended on two levels. One, that I didn't go to church, and two, that I would broadcast it on the network of T-shirt graphics. T-shirts are well known for being such a medium for communication. So I explained the marketing campaign.

I turned my back to reveal the phrase that was printed on the back of the shirt—again in bold yellow and a little larger font. It said "I am the church." The curl of a half smile appeared on her face, revealing that she understood the message. I went on to explain that I was on my way with some other people from my church to serve in the community.

"But it's Sunday morning," she replied, "shouldn't you be going to church?" I smiled and pointed to my chest with both fingers. "We don't go to church"; I said again, with emphasis. "We are the church!"

As money exchanged hands, I realized our conversation would be ending soon, so I quickly relayed that we were engaged in our annual Church without Walls (CWOW) weekend. I explained that one weekend every fall we cancel all our weekend services (Saturday night and Sunday morning) to mobilize our church family to serve in our community. Individuals, families, life groups, and other collective forces from our congregation select and fulfill a service project during the weekend. So instead of going to church for a *service*, we're out being the church by *serving*.

"I think that's great," she said.

"Thank you," I replied, "so do I."

This CWOW idea was certainly not original with our church. In fact, churches all over have been doing this sort of thing for a long time. But when we caught on to the concept of making a bold statement and providing a tangible illustration of what the church is really supposed to be, it began to get some real traction in our church family. On the weekend that followed CWOW, we celebrated our stories, and I shared that my dream for our church was that being a church without walls would become the regular heartbeat of our church. I suggested that maybe someday we wouldn't even need to do a CWOW weekend because we would all be living a CWOW lifestyle. We would be the church every day of life and everywhere we went. And we would never simply go to church again.

We also began to incorporate this new language into our church lexicon. People would approach me on the weekend and say, "Hey Dave (remember, "Just call me Dave"), guess how I was being the church this week?"

With genuine interest and excitement I would reply, "I'd love to hear how you were being the church."

They would go on to say how they had prepared a meal for a new mom or raked some leaves for an elderly widow with a yard full of mature maple trees. Or maybe they had brought in a gourmet coffee for a less-than-amicable coworker or insisted that some young parents let them entertain their three small children for an evening while the parents rediscovered what adult conversations and meals that don't include macaroni feel like again.

One of my favorite "being the church" stories was from a family in our church whose daughter was invited to a birthday party by one of her classmates. And let's just say the little girl who was having the party was not the most popular princess in this first-grade classroom. In fact, she came from a family that was pretty resource-challenged, and this unfortunate reality was reflected in her appearance as well. In spite of that, she distributed handmade invitations to all the other little girls in her class.

When the little girl from our church came home and showed her mother the invitation, she said, "I don't think anyone is going to her party, Mom. All the others girls said they weren't going."

To this her mother replied, "What do you think you should do, honey?"

Without hesitation she said, "Oh, I think I should go, even if no one else wants to."

And so the day of the party arrived, and this family from our church had decided that they would go a little above and beyond with the gift they would bring. They would get her a brand-new bike! And you may already have guessed, their daughter was the only one who responded to the invitation to come to the party. When they brought the new bicycle into the house, the birthday girl shrieked with joy. "I've always wanted a brand-new bicycle," she said. "And it's a girl's bike too!"

At some point after the traditional cake and candle rituals, it was time to leave the party. I don't remember if it was the mother or another relative, but as the family from our church was saying their good-byes to leave, this person followed them outside to thank them for coming. She expressed her anticipated concern for a complete no-show at the party. And then she asked them an unexpected question. "You guys go to that Tri-County Church, don't you?"

"Yes, we do," they replied.

"I thought so," she said. "You guys don't just go to church. You really show it."

They simply smiled and said, "Yeah, that's the way it's supposed to be."

That is the way it's supposed to be.

Jesus never intended for his church to be limited to a particular day when people gather in a building. He meant for us to go "outside the camp" (see the epigraph at the beginning of this chapter) the way he did as he gave his life away for the sake of others. Too many times church ends up being something people just go to and not something people are and do. Jesus had a number of ways of illustrating this profound truth.

More on this Salt-and-Light Business

In chapter seven, "It Looks a Lot like Love," I wrote about the need for proximity as it relates to loving people. Basically, you need to get close to people in order to love them. So logically, getting close enough to love people requires getting *out* from where you are and *out* to where they are. I'd like to revisit this business of salt and light as it relates to being a church without walls. As previously quoted, it is found in Jesus' Sermon on the Mount (Matthew 5:13-16).

You have probably heard many explanations for the salt and light in these familiar words of Jesus. But the simple and straightforward truth here is that for salt and light to be effective, they have to get *out* there. Maybe you've read one of the classic books on evangelism by Rebecca Manley Pippert, entitled, *Out of the Salt Shaker.* For salt to have its desired effect, it has to come in contact with the object of its influence. And for light to make any real difference at all, it has to be taken out of a place that's well lit and moved into the darkness. Salt in shakers and flashlights at midday never fulfill the purpose for which they were created.

And when I think about what happens at our church on the weekends, I get all salty and bright. I mean that in two ways. First, when believers gather corporately for worship, nurture, and inspiration, there's a lot of light in the room and a lot of salt in one place. And because we try to create welcoming environments and teach God's word in a culturally relevant and applicable way, it's a great environment for those who are still considering the way of Jesus. They can observe his love in us as we welcome them, and they can experience his truth at whatever particular place they happen to be at on the path. (I'll say more about that path in a moment.) Therefore, our weekend experience serves as a context for influencing and persuading those who come as seekers.

The second salt-and-light element of what happens on the weekends at Tri-County Church is that we are preparing and equipping people to go out of our services and building and into their everyday world—in other words, to go outside the camp. And in so doing, we are helping them to see that going to church on the weekend plays an important role in helping them to be the church in every other place and at every other time in their week. That is when we really get salt out of the shaker and take the light of Christ into the world. You never do that if all you ever do is go to church.

The LifePath

A little earlier I mentioned respecting the place people are in on their faith journey and where they're at along the "path." Well, the path is the way of Christ. To follow him and to become like him is God's desire for everyone, as I discussed in some detail in chapter six. And when churches recognize that, value that, and provide a system for that, it gets people moving—moving *onto* the path and *along* the path. We call it the *LifePath*.

The line pointing to the left is a movement away from God and his purpose for our lives. You might say, as well-known author and Senior Pastor of Willow Creek Church Bill Hybels says, that the people represented along that line are far from God. We have, in fact, adapted much of what we've learned in Willow Creek Church's REVEAL research into our strategy for spiritual formation. As you move from left to right, you encounter the first of four stick figures representing people on the path who are moving closer to God. This figure represents the person who is intentionally seeking spiritual truth, and we refer to this category as "exploring Christ."

Between this first person (I think they look like gingerbread people on our graphic) and the second one, there is the image of the cross. This represents the defining decision a person has made to follow Jesus. This is a critical moment, as it defines and empowers that person with the very Spirit of God, making that person a child of God and moving him or her forward along the LifePath in concert with other members of the family. And so this second figure—the first one to the right of the cross—is in the category we refer to as "new and growing in Christ." And like any newborn, people in this category depend on others for continued growth.

Next down the path is the person (with hands extended in both directions) who is growing deeper as a follower of Jesus. And the significance of the aforementioned outstretched arms is that they have an intentional connection with the person to the left—new and growing—and the person to their right, who is ahead of them on the LifePath. What chiefly characterizes this person is that he or she is spending time with God and engaging in his word on a regular basis, and this person has surrendered himself or herself to engaging in life together with other believers in community. One of the main purposes for engaging in life with those other people is to help the person make further progress along the path. Not surprisingly, we call those other people, collectively, "life groups." This third figure on the path represents the category we refer to as "close and growing in Christ."

The final of the four figures, located to the far right, is the Christ follower who has really found his or her groove. People in this group continue to grow deep in their relationship and reliance upon God and engaging in life with others and helping them along the LifePath. But in addition to that, they have narrowly defined their divine calling in life through the discovery and development of their spiritual gifts and are serving in what I like to call their "sweet spot." They often advance to leadership and equipping roles and, in some cases, begin new ministries and mission endeavors of their own. They not only see every member of God's family as a minister, but they also see that every member is also a missionary. We refer to the self-proclaimed missionaries in this category as "Christ-centered." And we all know what missionaries do—they go out!

And so people who are far from God get on the path as they follow Jesus and continue to follow Jesus in ever-increasing measure, always connected to the development of others to their right and left along the path. The LifePath arrow also extends indefinitely to the right because that progress toward Christ-centeredness is ongoing and that path always leads us back outside. Again the words of Hebrews chapter thirteen come to mind: "So let us go out to him, outside the camp, and bear the disgrace he bore."

That's why we call it a church without walls. Great and necessary things happen inside the walls of our church each weekend as we equip believers and welcome seekers. But the real engine of reaching people and changing lives is in the daily, normal, routine and yet strategic living of life as someone who is a fully devoted follower of Christ.

Get Out There and Don't Pull the Weeds

There's another place where Jesus speaks of the permeating influence of his kingdom *out there*. Read with discernment the following parable:

Here is another story Jesus told: "The Kingdom of Heaven is like a farmer who planted good seed in his field. But that night as the workers slept, his enemy came and planted weeds among the wheat, then slipped away. When the crop began to grow and produce grain, the weeds also grew. The farmer's workers went to him and said, 'Sir, the field where you planted that good seed is full of weeds! Where did they come from?' 'An enemy has done this!' the farmer exclaimed. 'Should we pull out the weeds?' they asked. 'No,' he replied, 'you'll uproot the wheat if you do. Let both grow together until the harvest. Then I will tell the harvesters to sort out the weeds, tie them into bundles, and burn them, and to put the wheat in the barn.'" (Matthew 13:24–30)

Do you see what Jesus is saying here? In addition to salt and light, Jesus is adding the metaphor of seeds and plants to illustrate the kingdom of God. And just like salt and light have to get out there to be effective, seeds have to get out there to grow. Naturally, they are sown among the same soil as other seeds and plants—those that represent people who are of the other kingdom, not God's. (See chapter one if you need a refresher on the specifics of these two competing kingdoms.) And *so* (pun intended) we *sow* these seeds as we live our lives as kingdom-of-God people in the presence of kingdom-of-this-world people. And Jesus says to just leave them growing together until the harvest.

Unfortunately, what the church has often been guilty of is gathering all the "God seeds" in one place—inside the walls of the church—and leaving all the "world seeds" outside the walls of the church. And this will continue to happen unless we become a church without walls. The soil we all live in is the same—this world and all the people in it. The difference is in the seeds. And we who have been born again of God's seed must be planted in the same soil, right alongside the other seeds that are still far from God.

Furthermore, our concern is not to be the distinction or the separation of these seeds. That is reserved for God alone at the time of the harvest. Our focus needs to be living out and growing the reflections of God's character in the very midst of these other weeds (to use Jesus' words). The wheat and the weeds must be allowed to grow together. Time will tell which is which. While they are young, wheat and weeds both look the same. Only God knows the difference. But unless we are living among those who are still far from God and showing them his love in consistent and tangible ways, they will never know there is another way to live—a better way to live. A life like the one Jesus lived.

Not Just Walls, but Gates Too

I remember hearing Rick Warren, of Saddleback Church and *The Purpose-Driven Life* fame, make the statement that hell is a gated community. This makes me laugh, because I actually live in a residential development that has a front and back gate. It's not so much that it's prestigious and exclusive; it was just originally designed as more of a recreational and resort community that eventually morphed into something more residentially conventional. But for all intents and purposes, it's a gated community too. I'm not saying that makes it hell. But I do live among the wheat and the weeds.

Here's the thing about gates: they're mostly to keep people out. If you belong in the gated community, you've got no issues with coming and going. But if you don't belong, that's another story. Tragically, church has not only erected walls historically, but they placed gates in the walls too. And those gates not only keep people who are far from God from coming in, but they also serve to keep the people of God from going out to be the witnesses Jesus calls us to be. As I mentioned in chapter five, Jesus never said to go witnessing. He said, "You will be my witnesses [out there] . . . in Jerusalem, Judea, Samaria and the uttermost parts." Do you get the same impression that I do—that those are all "out there" places? That you have to go outside the walls and the gates to go there? And so we've removed that gates that keep people out by welcoming them to "come as they are," and we've removed the walls to experience what it means to be the church everywhere else life takes us the rest of the week.

Now there's another bit of a snag. Evidently, hell is a gated community as well. Jesus said as much in his conversation with Peter about how he would build his church. Let's listen in: "Jesus replied, 'Blessed are you, Simon son of Jonah, for this was not revealed to you by man, but by my Father in heaven. And I tell you that you are Peter, and on this rock I will build my church, and the gates of Hades will not overcome it'" (Matthew 16:17–18 NIV).

So here's the way I see it. The kingdom of this world and hell is about gates—keeping people away from God and in bondage to sin. And the kingdom of God and heaven is about removing gates and walls, and even smashing through them if necessary. We who follow Jesus and are part of his church must be a church without walls. We must embrace fully the idea that the church is not a building but rather people—people that Christ is building. This includes people like Peter, who, in accepting the revelation that Jesus was the promised Messiah, became the rock upon which Christ would build his church.

I'll never forget the time when the church we planted in 1995 was about six months old and I ran into someone I knew from the previous church that I had served in as a youth pastor. This person asked me if we had started to build the church yet, and I quickly replied, "Yes!"

"Oh really," he said, "where are you building it?"

"Why, in DuBois," I said. "You know that's where we're living now."

"No, I mean where in DuBois are you building the church?"

I was beginning to get his drift, albeit I had for quite some time changed my thinking on churches and buildings. "Oh," I finally said, "You want to know if we've started constructing a building?" He seemed relieved that I was finally registering his question rightly, and with that I said, "Oh, not at all. We're probably a long way off from that. But we've been building the church from the very first day I arrived. That's because we are the church, and you don't necessarily need a church building to do that." In fact, we grew to a church of six hundred regular weekend attendees in three services before we got around to constructing our first permanent building—one of the locations we still meet in today.

I guess from that perspective we always have been a church without walls, because a church without a building is a church without walls and a church without gates. Jesus made one thing abundantly clear, and that was that while hell itself may have gates, it will not prevail against the overwhelming and permeating influence of God's kingdom here on earth. His kingdom is present even now. We've even been taught to pray for that: "Thy kingdom come . . ."

CHAPTER 10

THY KINGDOM COME

> Pray like this: "Our Father in heaven, may your name be kept holy.
> May your Kingdom come soon. May your will be done on earth as it is in heaven."
>
> —Matthew 6:9–10

As I begin writing this chapter, I happen to be sitting in the team meeting room of the Harmony House in the small, rural community of Harmons, Jamaica. Our church has been in a partnership for over a decade now with a mission organization known as Won by One to Jamaica, and we have been investing in this one area for a long period of time for a deeper and developmental impact. Planting a kingdom-minded church has been a part of those plans too.

The last thing needed in this community was another church. But I'm not talking about just another church. The island country of Jamaica has more churches per capita than almost any other place in the world. But like many places in the world, including our own country, much of what happens looks more like going to church than being the church. People dress up on Sunday and tote their Bibles to a building. They sing songs to and about God, and they listen to the "sage on the stage" deliver a message that is supposed to help them get a little closer to God.

And then comes Monday.

Maybe it doesn't even take that long. Even by Sunday afternoon, the church clothes come off and the songs you hear sound more like songs of stress and strife than praise and worship. In other words, church attendance has had no real impact on how lives are lived and people are loved. I see it in Jamaica, and I see it at home. We go through all the motions of piety and religious exercises, but there's not a deeper understanding of God's kingdom coming to earth or what that might look like if it did.

"Showing Clothes"

I was actually having a conversation about this during my time in Harmons with one of the Jamaicans that helps with the cooking while the teams from the States are here. His name is Dean, and one of his responsibilities is to prepare the jerk chicken on the final night of the trip. He also roasts fresh coffee—a pound or two of which also accompanies me on my trip back to Pennsylvania. I'll be honest, the real reason I was chatting with Dean is because I wanted to be near the jerk barrel and take in the amazing aroma that was creeping out of the perfectly seasoned wood-fired canister we were standing beside.

As we were comparing notes about how some people go to church every Sunday but continue to live selfish lives that lack love, he said to me, "Pasta Dave, wen people do dat, dey jus' showin' clothes, mon." And even with his distinctive Jamaican English, I knew exactly what he meant. "Showing clothes." It's another euphemism for *going* to church. People put on their Sunday best, as we like to say, and attend a church service in a church building, and they embrace something traditional and cultural rather than something transformational.

I don't want to be too harsh about this, as I believe that we're all recovering hypocrites to some extent. But if in addition to showing clothes we're not also showing Jesus to others by how we live and love every other day of the week, then we're guilty of the same thing that prompted the rebuke from Jesus toward the religious leaders of his day: "Everything they do is for show. On their arms they wear extra wide prayer boxes with Scripture verses inside, and they wear robes with extra long tassels. And they love to sit at the head table at banquets and in the seats of honor in the synagogues. They love to receive respectful greetings as they walk in the marketplaces, and to be called 'Rabbi'" (Matthew 23:5–7).

They were "showing clothes."

I guess that's one of the reasons we've taken a more casual approach to clothing in our church and broadcast a more come-as-you-are invitation to our weekend guests. A lot of people feel uncomfortable about even checking out church because they don't have the right clothes. This is even more the case in Jamaica, as I have observed it. It was the same kind of invitation Jesus offered to the people of his day. They too were weary of being not good enough and not clean enough and not well-dressed enough to be included in God's agenda.

But that was all about to change.

Jesus Preached the Kingdom

I began this book by establishing some thoughts about the reality of two competing kingdoms—God's and the world's—and alluded to the resurgence of the one true and legitimate kingdom. The entire Bible is the story of this kingdom, and it reaches its climax and simultaneously begins its catalytic final surge in the person of Jesus Christ. It's because of the kingdom of God that he came.

And Jesus didn't come to this earth to establish a religion or to get people to go to church. He came to reestablish God's kingdom. And you have to be a king to do that—make that *the* King. As discussed in earlier chapters, Jesus had to first deal with the estrangement between God and man caused by the original sin—which, simply stated, was man's decision to establish his own kingdom and willfully abandon the kingdom of God. And God, in his mercy, would send Jesus to earth to handle that matter by dying on the cross.

It was the cross that satisfied God's justice and made complete the remedy to our need for forgiveness. But it was the resurrection of Christ that assured us of new life and ushered mankind back into a relationship with God. This new life in the Spirit is about once again becoming God's children, heirs to his promises, and royal subjects of his kingdom. This kingdom would be reestablished in the incarnation, crucifixion, and resurrection of Jesus Christ. When Jesus came near, so did the kingdom of God.

The Kingdom of God Is Among You

The primary topic of Jesus' formal teaching was about the kingdom of God. He taught mostly in parables—stories about daily life to illustrate spiritual principles—and most of these parables were about the kingdom. He also made consistent statements about the kingdom being near, and present, and among.

At the very beginning of Jesus' teaching and ministry, he spoke of this reality: "Later on, after John was arrested, Jesus went into Galilee, where he preached God's Good News. 'The time promised by God has come at last!' he announced. 'The Kingdom of God is near! Repent of your sins and believe the Good News!'" (Mark 1:14–15).

And similarly, Matthew 3:2 states, "Repent of your sins and turn to God, for the Kingdom of Heaven is near." It was because Jesus was near them that the kingdom was near, and it was because Jesus was among them that the kingdom was among them. In fulfilling the primary purpose of his first coming, Jesus would provide the payment for sin so that they could in fact repent (turn away) from their sin to live this new life, this different way of living—kingdom living.

This new way of living would be characterized in the way Jesus lived his life, and it would be actualized in those who followed him and would eventually be filled with his Spirit. And a big part of what it meant to repent was to change their minds about what it means to be right with God. Instead of it being about the law (think *going* to church), it would be an inaugurated kingdom of God brought about by Jesus in his first coming, and it would be continued and extended through his followers (that's *being* the church) after his departure. On the day of Pentecost, when the Holy Spirit filled the believers, the kingdom would transition from being *near* and *among* them to being *in* and *through* them. Jesus referred to this new way of thinking as being "born again."

Born Again to What?

For those of us in the church, the whole idea of being "born again" is a pretty big deal. Traditionally the understanding has been that a person surrenders his or her life back to God, accepting his forgiveness, and then experiences a supernatural and spiritual rebirth—death to the old life and resurrection to the new, as it were. And what seems to have been the predominant rationale for this is the notion that we want to go to heaven and rather than to hell. But I believe there's a bit more going on here and that it's not just about being ready for a future eternal reality, but also about being included in a present eternal reality—a kingdom reality. Look again at this iconic passage related to the new birth:

There was a man named Nicodemus, a Jewish religious leader who was a Pharisee. After dark one evening, he came to speak with Jesus. "Rabbi," he said, "we all know that God has sent you to teach us. Your miraculous signs are evidence that God is with you." Jesus replied, "I tell you the truth, unless you are born again, you cannot see the Kingdom of God." "What do you mean?" exclaimed Nicodemus. "How can an old man go back into his mother's womb and be born again?" Jesus replied, "I assure you, no one can enter the Kingdom of God without being born of water and the Spirit. Humans can reproduce only human life, but the Holy Spirit gives birth to spiritual life. So don't be surprised when I say, 'You must be born again.'" (John 3:1–7)

Did you notice that Jesus says nothing here about going to heaven or not going to hell when you die? What he actually speaks to is "seeing" the kingdom. Being born again is not really so much about getting to heaven as it is about seeing the kingdom of God—and even more so, entering it. Please understand that I'm not denying that future destination and reality; I'm actually looking forward to it and understand completely the urgent nature of people "seeing" the kingdom before they die. But what I think Jesus is really trying to get across to Nicodemus here is that it's a spiritual transformation that leads to godly character and insight. It is a present reality that recognizes God's kingdom in the here and now. A person who is born again of the Spirit sees the world differently—not just in light of God's truth with reference to who he is and what we're all about, but also with respect to recognizing and participating in his kingdom, which is both present now and yet to come. And when a person lives that way, that person becomes a part of "Thy kingdom come, Thy will be done, on earth as it is in heaven."

For much of my Christian life, I have understood being born again as the password for getting to heaven when I die. But how much more glorious is the reality that this divinely-inspired spiritual transformation is the ability to *see* and participate in the very present and powerful kingdom of God. And I get to be a part of making it more visible to others—and by others I mean both those being loved and those who observe the loving. You've got to believe it to see it. It helps me to wake up every morning of my life seeing the kingdom and giving myself to the King's agenda. I think it's what Jesus was instructing his disciples to pray for every day.

The Lord's Prayer

I've always believed that when Jesus taught his disciples the Lord's Prayer, it was more a prescription for living than just a recitation for praying. It certainly includes all the necessary elements for a well-balanced prayer life—but then again, that's my point. Prayer is life. Our life is a prayer—or at least I think it's supposed to be. And so the Lord's Prayer is the way Jesus points us to what's really important, and what the agenda of God's purposes and desires (his kingdom) are all about. My purpose here is not to dissect these elements in their entirety, but to focus on the three primary phrases I've emphasized in bold in the following passage: "Our Father in heaven, may your name be kept holy. *May your Kingdom come soon. May your will be done on earth, as it is in heaven.* Give us today the food we need, and forgive us our sins, as we have forgiven those who sin against us. And don't let us yield to temptation, but rescue us from the evil one" (Matthew 6:9–13, emphasis mine).

Thy Kingdom Come

This is what God desires. This is what Jesus instructs his disciples to pray for. This is what it means to *be* the church. And while the notion of God's kingdom coming includes the idea of Jesus' return, when he will bring with him the creation of a new heaven and a new earth, he's also referring to the reality of the actual presence of God in the world, operating through his Spirit living in and through the lives of his people, the church. This will mark the culmination and full-force fruition of God's kingdom and the reign of Christ that is yet to come. But we must also recognize that the present reality of God's visible presence and power in the world is also in play here.

God's kingdom comes when Jesus comes. When those who follow Jesus come, God's kingdom comes. When people who love God with all their heart simultaneously love their neighbor, God's kingdom comes. When justice is brought to bear on injustice, God's kingdom comes. When the freedom of truth is unleashed on the bondage of error, God's kingdom comes. When forgiveness is chosen over vengeance, God's kingdom comes. When it looks a lot like love, God's kingdom comes.

And we are the ones who bring it!

Thy Will Be Done

The answer to the question of why the church exists lies in this second element. For the kingdom of God to come, it is assumed that the *will* of God will also be *done*. And so if the church isn't doing the will of God, it's not really the church after all. We see this contrast in the story from Adam to Jesus—from creation to incarnation. If you go all the way back to the creation, you can rediscover God's original intent. I won't repeat the larger treatment of this idea since I already examined it in some detail in chapter one. But suffice it to say that what man looked like in the garden before sin entered the world can easily be considered God's will, done. We were created for a relationship with God and were made in his image to reflect his character and his purposes. And you don't get very far in the book of Genesis before that gets royally messed up. Think about it: In Genesis chapters one and two, God creates and it's all good. In Genesis chapter three, all hell breaks loose. Seriously—we only get to chapter three?

Okay, fast forward to Bethlehem. God becomes a man. Heaven comes to earth. And this time, in the person of God's one and only Son, Jesus, we get a picture of what God's original intention for man was all along. Jesus was, in human form, the very representation of God, and what God had purposed in his mind for all of us.

Christ is the visible image of the invisible God. He existed before anything was created and is supreme over all creation, for through him God created everything in the heavenly realms and on earth. He made the things we can see and the things we can't see—such as thrones, kingdoms, rulers, and authorities in the unseen world. Everything was created through him and for him. He existed before anything else, and he holds all creation together. Christ is also the head of the church, which is his body. He is the beginning, supreme over all who rise from the dead. So he is first in everything. For God in all his fullness was pleased to live in Christ, and through him God reconciled everything to himself. He made peace with everything in heaven and on earth by means of Christ's blood on the cross. (Colossians 1:15–20)

What was started and lost in Genesis was restarted and found in Jesus. He is the visible image of the invisible God, and he is also the head of the church, which is his body. And everything that Jesus did was according to his Father's will. He said he came to do the will of the one who sent him, and on the night before his crucifixion, as he faced the most agonizing element of his earthly mission, he consigned himself yet again to the Father's will:

Then Jesus went with them to the olive grove called Gethsemane, and he said, "Sit here while I go over there to pray." He took Peter and Zebedee's two sons, James and John, and he became anguished and distressed. He told them, "My soul is crushed with grief to the point of death. Stay here and keep watch with me." He went on a little farther and bowed with his face to the ground, praying, "My Father! If it is possible, let this cup of suffering be taken away from me. Yet I want your will to be done, not mine." (Matthew 26:36–39)

You do realize what that means, don't you? The implication is that as his body, the church, we are also to be the visible image of the invisible God. As we follow Jesus (our head and leader) in the power of his indwelling and image-reflecting Spirit, we, the church, become the visible presence of God in this world—yes, this broken, fallen, world. And it is only as we reflect his character and do his will that his presence and power become visible on this earth. And so the kingdom of God *comes* through Jesus and the will of God is *done* through Jesus. It makes sense, then, that when we follow Jesus in the power of his Spirit, we both bring the kingdom and do the will of God as well. The only other question is *where*. Where do we bring his kingdom and do his will? On earth, silly.

On Earth as It Is in Heaven

I think I spent a significant portion of my early journey with God with the understanding that the mission of the church was to get people to heaven. You know—share the gospel, lead them in the prayer, and get them to *go* to church. I now see that as being good-hearted but misguided. It seems very clear to me now, especially in light of the Lord's Prayer, that it's really more about getting heaven to people than it is getting people to heaven. Take nothing away from the firm hope of every believer in a preferred future when God's kingdom will be in full operation. But what about right *now*—and until *then*?

On one of my first trips to Jamaica, I was introduced to the marvelous culture of Jamaican song, and much of that culture is immersed in the music of the church. There's one song in particular that always comes to my mind, and it reflects the joyful anticipation of one day experiencing our perfect, sorrow-free home in heaven. But it also perpetuates the idea of getting people to heaven rather than getting heaven to people. The lyrics are as follows:

> Won't it be a time, when we get over yonder,
> Won't it be a time, when we get over yonder,
> Won't it be a time, when we get over yonder.
> Oh, won't it be a time . . .

Now I totally get how these kinds of songs and this mentality are formed out of the hopelessness and despair of many cultures of poverty and oppression. And one begins to wonder if God's only plan for relieving such suffering will play out only after one leaves this planet. But what if God showed up in places of need and deprivation in the form of his people filled with his love, committed to doing his will? As a pastor, I often hear people ask why God doesn't see all this suffering and do something about it. But maybe God is thinking, "I do see what you see. What are you doing about it? Have you considered the idea that I want to send you as a way of sending me?"

Being the church as opposed to just going to church is about recognizing that God does see what's going on in the world and sends us out (remember the church without walls?) to do something about it. In fact, in the one place in the New Testament that Jesus speaks specifically to the issue of where we go when this life is over (Matthew 25:31–46), he refers to it in terms of feeding hungry people, offering drink to thirsty people, visiting the infirm and imprisoned, and clothing the naked. He said that when we do those kinds of things, we're doing them to him.

There's a profound implication here, because I used to think that when I was involved in this sort of compassionate activity, I was bringing Jesus to the people in need. But I think a more accurate understanding is that when we love and care for those in great need, we are simply joining Jesus; he is already with them. When we go to them, we "see" Jesus. When we love them, we are also loving Jesus. And when we love them, Jesus is loving them through us. That's why the Great Commandment includes loving your neighbor as yourself and not just loving God with all your heart. God does see what's happening on the earth. He wants us to see it too and bring his kingdom and his will to impact it. His *kingdom* come. His *will* be done. On *earth* as it is in heaven.

"Do This . . ."

I'm not sure if you've ever considered this, but I think this is exactly what Jesus was getting at on the night before he went to the cross as he celebrated the Passover with his disciples. There was a lot going on that night around the table—the washing of feet, the hushed discussion of a betrayer, Jesus' words of comfort about going to prepare a place, and so on. But there was also the symbolism of the bread and the cup. Most of us who are accustomed to the practices of the church know this as Communion or the Lord's Table. It's a powerful and sacred ceremony—but perhaps not for all the reasons you assume. Let's revisit the first time this happens:

When the time came, Jesus and the apostles sat down together at the table. Jesus said, "I have been very eager to eat this Passover meal with you before my suffering begins. For I tell you now that I won't eat this meal again until its meaning is fulfilled in the Kingdom of God." Then he took a cup of wine and gave thanks to God for it. Then he said, "Take this and share it among yourselves. For I will not drink wine again until the Kingdom of God has come." He took some bread and gave thanks to God for it. Then he broke it in pieces and gave it to the disciples, saying, "This is my body, which is given for you. *Do this to remember me.*" After supper he took another cup of wine and said, "This cup is the new covenant between God and his people—an agreement confirmed with my blood, which is poured out as a sacrifice for you." (Luke 22:14–20, emphasis mine)

So then, Jesus begins celebrating the Passover the way God's people had done for centuries—ever since the original Passover itself, when God spared all the firstborn sons of Israel from the angel of death, who was sent upon their Egyptian captors. It's not my purpose to detail all the amazing parallels found in the Passover meal and the person of Jesus, but let me just say that Jesus was making it really personal on this night. This truly was a night like no other.

And so, for centuries following this "Last Supper," believers have celebrated the bread and the cup to remember the sacrificial death of God's one and only Son for the sin of mankind. The bread represents his body, given for us; and the wine represents his blood, poured out for us. And Jesus says, as we eat the bread and drink of the cup, "Do this in remembrance of me." And we do. We celebrate communion to remember what Jesus has done for us through the cross—purchased our pardon and restored us to a relationship with God.

But what if this ceremony is more than just remembering *what* Jesus has done for us? What if it's also about remembering *why* Jesus has done this for us? Remembering *what* he did is about our forgiveness being accomplished on the cross. He gave his body and he poured out his blood. Remembering *why* he did this is about him giving his life to us and extending his mission through us. He died so that we could be forgiven. He rose to live again so that we could live again (be born again) as well. So is it possible that when Jesus said, "Do this," he was referring to something in addition to remembering his death? Is there also an implication and a foretelling of his resurrection?

Think for a moment about what's involved in remembrance. When we remember someone, we recount and celebrate the things the person did and what he or she was all about. Appropriately, we do that with Jesus when we observe Communion. But don't we also remember and honor people in an even more significant way when we carry on their legacy, their mission, and all the things they represented? Charles Colton once said that imitation is the sincerest form of flattery, and what could be more honoring and memorializing of Jesus than to extend his legacy, his mission, and everything he represented? Perhaps that's also what he meant by "Do this."

For example, Jesus broke the bread, passed it around, and said it represented his body. Then the disciples ate the bread. Where does bread go when you eat it? Inside you, of course. Jesus divided the bread among them, and it went inside them—just the way the Holy Spirit goes inside anyone who believes in Christ. The bread is his body in us, and we become his body. Likewise, he blessed the cup of wine, and they drank it. He said it represented his blood, which is poured out as a sacrifice for us. The disciples drank the wine. Where did the wine go? Where everything you've ever had to drink goes—inside you. We are his body and we have been saved by his blood. Now that he is in us and flows through us, what does that mean? It means to "do this."

In essence, Jesus is saying this: "In the same way that I have given my life away for the sake of others, and have poured out my blood for the *benefit* of others, I want you to give your life away and pour out your life for others too. I want you to live the way you saw me live. I want you to love the way you saw me love. I want you to give away your life in selfless love toward others (as I'm doing with my body), and I want you to pour out your life in service to others (as I'm doing with my blood)." I think the apostle Paul may have been seeing it this way when he wrote this in Philippians 2:17: "But I will rejoice even if I lose my life, pouring it out like a liquid offering to God, just like your faithful service is an offering to God." What else could this possibly mean?

Daily Bread

I'm convinced, then, as I hope you may also be, that when Jesus said, "Do this," he was not simply telling us to remember with regularity what he did on the cross. How could you ever forget that anyway? And while I think it certainly includes that, and that it's a precious practice shared by believers when they gather, I believe that Jesus is also telling us that the most significant way to remember him is by keeping his kingdom's agenda alive and active. And how often should we "do this"? How often should we give our bodies and pour out our lives for the sake of others? Does the expression "daily bread" ring a bell?

Just a final thought on the "do this" of the Lord's Table. Regarding the observance of communion, the apostle Paul said, "For every time you eat this bread . . ." (1 Corinthians 11:26), implying more regularity than formality. This was a bread-eating culture. Usually, even if you didn't have anything else in the house to eat, you had some bread. Bread was sustenance. Bread was life. And bread was every day. I think the reason Jesus chose bread as the reminder of what he did—and what we're supposed to do—was because the people of his time would have been reminded of those two things on a daily basis.

And so instead of a periodic or even weekly observance of a religious ordinance, it would have been (and perhaps should still be) a daily reminder of the Jesus way of life. I can imagine an early first century Christian family as they sat down to share in their evening meal—perhaps their only meal. The father or other head of the house would start by passing out bread. And when he broke that loaf—as he had done the day before and would do the day after—he might ask, "You all know what this is, right? This is the body of our Lord, Jesus, who gave himself for us so that we could be forgiven and have new life in his Spirit. And this new life allows us to live our lives for him as we give our lives in love to others. We are his body now. He lives through us now. And until he comes back, we *do this* . . ."

"Greater Things Shall You Do"

When Jesus served his final Passover meal to his disciples, he said that he would not "eat this meal" or "drink this wine" until its meaning was fulfilled in the kingdom of God. He is coming back someday, you know. But that much-anticipated return seems to be contingent on us "doing this" and "being the church" until he comes. Unbelievably, he even suggests that we can accomplish more as his collective body, the church, than he could accomplish in his solitary earthly body. I think that may be what Jesus is saying in the following passage: "Very truly I tell you, whoever believes in me will do the works I have been doing, and they will do even *greater* things than these, because I am going to the Father" (John 14:12, emphasis mine).

Yes, Jesus leaves to go to the Father. But Jesus leaves something behind—his church. All those who find new life and follow Jesus perpetuate the kingdom of God in exponential ways. Jesus knew what he was doing when he was forming his disciples, and he knew how to extend the agenda of God's kingdom when he commanded us to go into all the world and make them. It would be through us, his body, as we continued to "do this" and "be the church" (rather than just "go to church") that his kingdom would come and his will would be done on earth as it is in heaven.

Even so, Lord Jesus, come quickly.

CHAPTER 11

FINALLY HOME

> Then I saw a new heaven and a new earth, for the old heaven and the old earth had disappeared. And the sea was also gone. And I saw the holy city, the new Jerusalem, coming down from God out of heaven like a bride beautifully dressed for her husband. I heard a loud shout from the throne, saying, "Look, God's home is now among his people! He will live with them, and they will be his people. God himself will be with them. He will wipe every tear from their eyes, and there will be no more death or sorrow or crying or pain. All these things are gone forever."
>
> —Revelation 21:1–4

Have you ever been away from home—perhaps a long distance from home—and it seemed as if it were taking forever to finally get home? The feeling gets even more amplified when you're traveling in a car with four small children. At an earlier time in our lives, we had four under the age of five, and I can assure you we had some memorable, and sometimes intolerable, returns to home.

But a more recent example for me is a trip I took with the executive pastor on staff with me at our church. We were invited on a vision trip with Compassion International, to the country of Uganda. We have partnered with Compassion for years and were delighted to see firsthand the incredible work for the kingdom they do in this country—and all over the world, for that matter. In any case, we were really far from home—as far as I have ever been in my lifetime.

Did I mention that I'm not a good flyer?

Suffice it to say that after a memorable and inspirational journey, it was finally time to head for home. Let me review that travel itinerary for you: We had been in Kenya for the final day of our trip and arrived at the Nairobi airport to what I can only describe as utter chaos. We had been standing in the check-in line for over an hour and were just about to approach the agent when a security officer who was trying to manage an ever-increasing situation of overcrowding moved us to another line. And, of course, the computer wasn't working and we were stalled for another hour. So what had begun as ample time, even for an international flight, had eroded into my own personal panic about making our flight to Amsterdam.

Thankfully, and miraculously I might add, we boarded the plane just before gate closing, and I breathed a sigh of relief as I leaned back for our eight-hour overnight flight to the Netherlands. After arriving, we had a five-hour layover before we boarded for another eight-hour leg to Detroit, Michigan. Now, if you remember, I'm from Pennsylvania, not Michigan. Landing in Detroit found us making our way to a flight to Pittsburgh—closer, but not home yet. When we landed in Pittsburgh, barely sane and beyond exhausted, we got into the car for a two-hour drive home to DuBois, Pennsylvania. Those two hours seemed like two more days. But I remember well the turn signals flashing and ticking, indicating that we were finally home.

There's no feeling quite like being finally home.

Now, imagine for a moment that this life God has granted us—and even the whole of his historical dealings with all mankind—is like a long journey far from home. Then you can see what a similarly comforting and joyous experience will be ours when we are finally home in the spiritual sense. We will feel the way we have all felt when we have finally returned home from a long and far-away journey. We'll feel as though we have gotten back to where we truly belong. We will have experienced nothing so wonderful as it in our lifetime on earth. And this ultimate homecoming will include the re-creation of a new heaven and a new earth, just as the passage from Revelation chapter one that I cited at the beginning of this chapter indicates. It will all be new!

"Dwell in the house of the Lord forever"

Another insight to this idea of returning to God's original plan can be found in one of the most recognized and memorized passages in the Bible—the twenty-third psalm. In the sixth and final verse of this treasured poem, King David speaks of the future reality of eternal life in the presence of God. And everyone who has ever committed this passage to memory, which we all seem to do using the King James Version, uses the word "dwell" to describe activity in this heavenly reality. But a brilliant Hebrew professor from my seminary days—and truly one of the best teachers I've ever sat under—one day pointed out in class that the word translated as "dwell" or "live" here in Psalm 23:6 is actually translated from the Hebrew word "*shuv*," which means "return."

Quite literally, then, David is saying that he will "return" to the house of the Lord, forever. And while the difference between dwelling and returning may seem insignificant—I mean, after all, as long as we end up in the same place, right?—I value the implications of "return" over "dwell." For to return to the house of the Lord implies that I am going back to a place and a position that I've always belonged to but have yet to arrive at, much like returning from a long journey away from home—you know, being finally home.

If you think about it, this is also what drives all of Jesus' stories about reaching the *lost*. The most vital truth about those who are lost is that they belong somewhere else where they would be considered *found*—in other words, home. The understanding of the nature of being lost and its implications on the mission of reaching people and making disciples is helpfully labeled as "lostology" in a book called *Get Out of Their Faces and Into Their Shoes* by John Kramp. Though it was written some years ago, I still find it to be a great resource for living a missional life—and helping others find their way home.

And so, the one who finds his way back home—to where he belongs—is said to have *returned*, and in some cases to have been *found*. Which is exactly what happens to everyone who finds his or her way back to God through Jesus Christ. We are back where we belong. And then beyond that, on the day that our earthly life comes to a close, or the day when Jesus returns (the end of the world, you might say), we return to God's house, where we will dwell with him forever. And in that reality we are, in fact, finally home.

I am just now reminded of a wonderful statement made by A. W. Tozer in his classic book *The Pursuit of God*, where he says, "God was our original habitat and our hearts cannot but feel at home when they enter again that ancient and beautiful abode" (Kindle location 997).

Speaking of the End of the World

What many people refer to as the "end of the world" the Bible actually calls a new beginning—at least for those who have placed their faith in Jesus Christ. And with so many people seemingly obsessed with the topic, it presents those who follow Christ with a great opportunity to share the hope of this cosmic re-creation.

For example, I remember the time someone spent an unbelievable amount of money on a national advertising campaign that claimed that the end of the world would take place that year on May 21. It was on billboards, newspapers, and the Internet. There was even a maroon Cadillac parked along a major thoroughfare in our community covered with yellow decals, promoting this soon-coming event. And as has happened with many other prognostications of the return of Christ, the day came and went. I think it was recalculated for October. I didn't hold my breath for that one either.

I remember referring to this from the pulpit that weekend in May, before it was to take place, and I said this: "What if he's right? I mean, I know the Bible says we're not supposed to speculate about this and that only the Father knows the day and the hour, but what if out of sheer coincidence this guy got it right? What's that mean for all of us?"

I went on to point out that in some respect he would indeed be right—for some, but not for all. What I meant was that the end of the world happens every day for some people. To be more precise, about 152,000 people die every day on our planet, and their world, to be sure, comes to an end. So the real issue isn't about when the world is coming to an end, but rather whether we are ready for it when it happens—especially if it happens today. This is where the urgency and the importance of the gospel of Jesus Christ come into full view. God wants us to be prepared and to be a part of that wonderful re-creation he is planning at the end of time as we know it. And the Bible is very clear that it is God's grace toward us—and our belief in him—that secures our future destiny in this heaven and earth that are new. What I'm trying to say is that we have to be a part of his kingdom now if we are to be a part of it then.

Coming or Going?

As one who has grown up in the church, having decided to follow Christ as a child, I, like many, have speculated about where heaven is and what heaven is like. Heaven was always somewhere I was going to go when I die, and it was somewhere distant from where I was. But a closer examination of Revelation 21 paints a different picture. Look again with me at these verses: "Then I saw a new heaven and a new earth, for the old heaven and the old earth had disappeared. And the sea was also gone. And I saw the holy city, the new Jerusalem, coming down from God out of heaven like a bride beautifully dressed for her husband. I heard a loud shout from the throne, saying, 'Look, God's home is now among his people! He will live with them, and they will be his people. God himself will be with them'" (Revelation 21:1–3).

Do you notice that this new heaven and new earth—including the new Jerusalem—was coming *down* out of heaven? And further, do you notice that God's home (which we typically think of as heaven) is now among his people—that he will now live with *them*? What does this description remind you of? When did God once live with his people? During their time in the garden, of course, when we read about him walking and talking with our first parents in the cool of the day. In other words, God will bring everything back to the way it was originally before sin entered the world. And the big adjustment for my thinking on this topic is that we're not really going somewhere else to join God in heaven; rather, he's coming back to be with us. He will *be* with us and he will *live* with us, and we will live with him. What a glorious day that will be! Can you even imagine it?

Resurgent Kingdom to Realized Kingdom

Let me recap a few thoughts so far. I have already built the case that *being* the church rather than *going* to church is about God's visible presence being lived out in the lives of his redeemed people, the church. And in living out these transformed lives of love, we are a part of bringing his kingdom to earth as it is in heaven. And the future reality that we who are participants in this "here and now" kingdom of God have to look forward to is that this *resurgent* kingdom of God will become the *realized* kingdom of God. We will return from an inaugurated kingdom of heaven to a fully-realized, back-to-the-original one.

So which is it? Do we go to heaven, or does heaven come to us? Even in pondering that question, our thinking is in alignment with heaven as a particular *place* rather than a particular *reality*. There's no question in my mind that heaven is a real, conscious, and eternal place, and I believe the same is true of hell. But what makes heaven, heaven is not the location, but the population—those who actually live there, and of course, the most important occupant of heaven: God himself. In all actuality, it matters little where heaven actually is as long God is living there among us. This is what Genesis chapter one says he did, and this is also what Revelation 21 says he will do again. Perhaps a clear explanation from Jesus himself is in order here.

On his last night with the disciples, as they faced some troubling uncertainties, Jesus shared these words with them: "Don't let your hearts be troubled. Trust in God, and trust also in me. There is more than enough room in my Father's home. If this were not so, would I have told you that I am going to prepare a place for you? When everything is ready, I will come and get you, so that you will always be with me where I am. And you know the way to where I am going" (John 14:1–4).

Notice that Jesus indeed refers to this future fulfillment as a place—a very real place. But he also clarifies what makes this place the promise that it will someday truly be: ". . . so that you will always be with me where I am." So being finally home, or going to heaven, is actually more about *who* will be with us in heaven than *where* heaven itself will be. That's why he's coming back—so that he can live with us again as it was in the beginning.

Have you ever wondered what life was like on the earth and for our first parents before the fateful day of their self-declared independence?

A Future Hope and Home

Another very familiar Old Testament passage speaks of this homecoming. It is found in the letter the prophet Jeremiah wrote to the Israelites who were taken into captivity by the Babylonians and King Nebuchadnezzar. Also prophesying during the outset of this captivity were false prophets who were telling the people that the exile would only last a short time, that it would all be over in a couple of years. But Jeremiah refutes them and gives the captives a clearer picture of their future.

This is what the LORD says: "You will be in Babylon for seventy years. But then I will come and do for you all the good things I have promised, and I will bring you home again. For I know the plans I have for you," says the LORD. "They are plans for good and not for disaster, to give you a future and a hope. In those days when you pray, I will listen. If you look for me wholeheartedly, you will find me. I will be found by you," says the LORD. "I will end your captivity and restore your fortunes. I will gather you out of the nations where I sent you and will bring you home again to your own land." (Jeremiah 29:10–14)

If you're familiar with this passage, then you know that it happened exactly as Jeremiah (or God, rather) said it would. And though these words of hope and restoration were indeed for this particular time and circumstance—as is much of God's prophetic word in Scripture—it contains a broader, more inclusive application as well.

Did you notice the "bring you home" language of this text? God did, in fact, bring his people back home to Jerusalem, though it was in shambles. And he would later raise up a regular guy named Nehemiah to rebuild the walls of Jerusalem both literally and spiritually—but that's another story for another time. What I find inspiring about this account is that Jeremiah, speaking for God, tells them that they're going to be there for seventy years—essentially a lifetime, if you will—and that they should just settle in, settle down, and live life. Specifically, God instructs them as follows: "This is what the LORD of Heaven's Armies, the God of Israel, says to all the captives he has exiled to Babylon from Jerusalem: 'Build homes, and plan to stay. Plant gardens, and eat the food they produce. Marry and have children. Then find spouses for them so that you may have many grandchildren. Multiply! Do not dwindle away! And work for the peace and prosperity of the city where I sent you into exile. Pray to the LORD for it, for its welfare will determine your welfare'" (Jeremiah 29:4–7).

God is basically saying that even though this exile is temporary (about the length of an average lifetime), he wants them to go on living. And not just living, but prospering. And there's even the idea that their trust in God and faith in his presence and provision in this foreign land will have a spiritual impact on their foreign hosts. Okay, maybe "host" is a mild way to put it. But amazingly, God is doing something missional and purposeful even in the midst of this captivity.

And in a previously cited example, in his being uprooted from his homeland—to journey through a wilderness of exile and then to be finally taken back to a promised land—the calling and mission of Abraham to be blessed in order to bless other nations is in play here as well. We see the same theme in the exodus too. God takes his people from a place that's not really their home (Egypt), through a wilderness journey that pastor and author Jeff Manion refers to in his wonderful book *The Land Between*. This land between is a time of exile that prepares God's people to truly be God's people when we finally arrive in the Promised Land. It is, in reality, our life on earth. We are exiles and nomads, and even as we sojourn, we learn to trust God and show his power and glory to others along the way. It's also the primary mission of the church—to live in and pray for the city God has us dwelling in right now, in order to reveal God to those who still don't know him.

So here's my connection to the broader application. Most of us are given roughly seventy years in a place that really isn't our home. We, too, are living as exiles in a foreign land. And for that lifetime that God has granted us in this land that really isn't our true home, he wants us to live life—a life of faith and following him. And as we're living that life of living like Jesus and loving like Jesus—in the city that we're being held "captive" in—we are to pray for and work toward peace with those with whom we live (yes, even if they're very different from us or even hostile toward us). Or, to put it in the vernacular of this book, they were *being* the church instead of just *going* to church. And subsequently, the people we live among in our city will stand to benefit as well.

And then, when this lifetime God has given us comes to its earthly conclusion, we, like the Israelites returning from Babylon, will be brought home to God's good plan of ending our captivity and restoring our fortunes. He's talking about the new heaven and the new earth and the New Jerusalem. And that's when we'll be finally home again.

And I think we'll be thirty-three again too.

Thirty-Three Again

Okay, I'd like to dream a little bit with you right now. Where I'm going with a few of my thoughts may be a little speculative—but I think you may agree that they are not without some scriptural implication and perhaps even some substantiation. For starters, I think we'll all be thirty-three again. Yes, you read correctly: thirty-three! Now, I know you love the idea of that, especially if you're already beyond those years in real life. I am almost fifty-two years old as of this writing, and while I'm thankful to be in good health, I don't kid myself by believing I can do what I could do in my early thirties.

I have a couple of factors for my thirty-three theory. First of all, as most of us know, Jesus lived to the age of thirty-three. His earthly ministry officially commenced when he was thirty, and he was crucified three years later. It's safe to assume that the body he had in his postresurrection appearances—although glorified and eternal—would have been of the same stature and likeness that he had possessed just three days prior.

The second notion along these lines is in Genesis, when God creates man from the dust and woman from man's rib. He fashioned them as full-grown adults rather than children or adolescents. And it makes logical sense that, prior to sin, God's plan for them involved neither aging nor death. I'm guessing that Adam and Eve, on day one of creation, looked to be about thirty-three years old—or maybe I should say "young." Oh yeah, I'm still not sure if Adam had a belly button or not.

One final suggestion in support of my idea comes from one of my favorite pastimes—watching NFL football. I also have a son who played football in high school and college, and I'll be honest, I loved watching him play even more than I loved watching the professionals. But if we were to think logically about the age at which professional football players—or athletes of any other sports, for that matter—reach the prime of their career, I think many would agree that it's in their early thirties. They are not only fully and physically developed, but they have also reached the crescendo of experience and maturity in their field. But unfortunately, in the years that follow (32, 33, 34, etc.), the deceleration of performance begins, marking the beginning of the end for every professional athlete's career.

In my opinion, thirty-three is the prime of life. Oh, to be thirty-three again. I know this seems crazy, but I not only think that it's possible, I think it's probable—for those who experience new and eternal life in Christ. I think we're going to live forever with God and be thirty-three again. And on top of that, we'll finally be home again too!

Home Sweet Home

Another hallmark of what we consider the characteristics of being home again is the idea of peace and harmony. In an earlier chapter I spoke of the Hebrew idea of shalom, which we always translate into English as "peace." But if you recall, a more accurate translation of this biblical term is "completion" or "harmony." When everything is complete and working in harmony as it should, we experience peace. Likewise, when we finally return to living in the presence of God—when everything has been restored to its original completeness and harmony—we will experience the reality of those pre-sin days in the garden: perfect peace.

The Bible says that when God created Adam and immediately declared that it was not good that he was alone, God created the woman to complete him. Additionally, Adam was not made complete simply by receiving the woman from God. Completeness came in the divine trilogy of the man, the woman, and God. What makes any individual or any marriage or any human enterprise compete by God's standard is God himself being in the mix. That's why God was there with them in the beginning as they enjoyed fellowship *together.* And that's why God is going to join us again in the new heaven and the new earth. It won't be so much a new thing as it will be a restoration of the original thing. Which again is why David says in Psalm 23, "I will return to the house of the Lord," and Jesus says in John 14, "I will come and get you so that you will always be with me where I am."

The writer of Hebrews speaks to this reality as well: "And just as each person is destined to die once and after that comes judgment, so also Christ died once for all time as a sacrifice to take away the sins of many people. He will come again, not to deal with our sins, but to bring salvation to all who are eagerly waiting for him" (Hebrews 9:27–28). A clear explanation is given here of the purpose of the first and second advent of Christ into the world. The first time Jesus came was to take away our sin. The second time will be to bring salvation to its ultimate fruition and his kingdom to its full and final realization. In other words, things will be complete again and operating as they were originally intended to by God. We will be home, sweet home, again.

A bit later, in Hebrews chapter 13:10–16 we read the following:

We have an altar from which the priests in the Tabernacle have no right to eat. Under the old system, the high priest brought the blood of animals into the Holy Place as a sacrifice for sin, and the bodies of the animals were burned outside the camp. So also Jesus suffered and died outside the city gates to make his people holy by means of his own blood. So let us go out to him, outside the camp, and bear the disgrace he bore. For this world is not our permanent home; we are looking forward to a home yet to come. Therefore, let us offer through Jesus a continual sacrifice of praise to God, proclaiming our allegiance to his name. And don't forget to do good and to share with those in need. These are the sacrifices that please God.

In these verses the writer speaks of the present and future kingdom. With reference to the future, he says that this world is not our home and that we look forward to a home yet to come—or, more accurately, to a return to our original home, sweet home. But the author is also aware of the present (already, not yet) kingdom of God and thus encourages us to continue to devote ourselves to following Jesus and living a life of loving others the way he did until he comes back. In other words, "Do this in remembrance of me" (as covered in the previous chapter).

The Lion and the Lamb

Jesus lives *in* us (his body, the church) here and now, and he will live once again *with* us (new heaven, new earth) then and there. The prophet Isaiah records a glorious picture of what this future reality possesses:

In that day the wolf and the lamb will live together; the leopard will lie down with the baby goat. The calf and the yearling will be safe with the lion, and a little child will lead them all.

The cow will graze near the bear. The cub and the calf will lie down together. The lion will eat hay like a cow. The baby will play safely near the hole of a cobra. Yes, a little child will put its hand in a nest of deadly snakes without harm. Nothing will hurt or destroy in all my holy mountain, for as the waters fill the sea, so the earth will be filled with people who know the LORD. (Isaiah 11:6–9)

This is a beautiful picture of peace, harmony, and completeness. It is also a picture of what life was like before sin inaugurated the competition between God's kingdom and the kingdom of this world. And sin always turns completion into competition. It corrupted everything in life, from marriage to the marketplace to relationships among the nations. But this competition is soon going to come to a conclusion, when God will put right all that has gone wrong, and things will again be as they were, and "the earth will be filled with people who know the Lord."

There is a sense in which the promise of this future reality and return to God's original intent assists us in enduring the far-from-complete world we still find ourselves living in on this side of Jesus' return:

All praise to God, the Father of our Lord, Jesus Christ. It is by his great mercy that we have been born again, because God raised Jesus Christ from the dead. Now we live with great expectation, and we have a priceless inheritance—an inheritance that is kept in heaven for you, pure and undefiled, beyond the reach of change and decay. And through your faith, God is protecting you by his power until you receive this salvation, which is ready to be revealed on the last day for all to see. So be truly glad. There is wonderful joy ahead, even though you have to endure many trials for a little while. These trials will show that your faith is genuine. It is being tested as fire tests and purifies gold—though your faith is far more precious than mere gold. So when your faith remains strong through many trials, it will bring you much praise and glory and honor on the day when Jesus Christ is revealed to the whole world. (1 Peter 1:3–7)

Peter assures those addressed in this letter to his persecuted brethren that they can remain truly glad because of the wonderful joy that lies ahead of them. When Christ finally returns (and us with him), he will reveal himself to the whole world, and we will be found among those who belong to him and share in his kingdom. And the one thing that has characterized his followers during their time on earth will be the only thing that carries over into the new heaven and new earth—and it looks a lot like love!

Only Love Lasts Forever

It's not surprising that I find myself returning to the theme of love at the conclusion of this book on *being* the church. What characterized Jesus' life on earth and our following him will also be the driving force in our life with him forever. When we think of all the possible places to understand love in the biblical sense, perhaps none comes to mind more quickly than 1 Corinthians 13—often referred to as the Love Chapter. And while this is most often recited in the context of wedding ceremonies, it is more contextually connected to what it means to *be* the church. And the church, not surprisingly, is also referred to as the bride of Christ. In describing what the church is in its essence, the defining word for Paul in this passage is "love."

If I could speak all the languages of earth and of angels, but didn't love others, I would only be a noisy gong or a clanging cymbal. If I had the gift of prophecy, and if I understood all of God's secret plans and possessed all knowledge, and if I had such faith that I could move mountains, but didn't love others, I would be nothing. If I gave everything I have to the poor and even sacrificed my body, I could boast about it; but if I didn't love others, I would have gained nothing. Love is patient and kind. Love is not jealous or boastful or proud or rude. It does not demand its own way. It is not irritable, and it keeps no record of being wronged. It does not rejoice about injustice but rejoices whenever the truth wins out. Love never gives up, never loses faith, is always hopeful, and endures through every circumstance. (1 Corinthians 13:1–7)

It shouldn't come as a huge surprise that 1 Corinthians 13 is sandwiched between two chapters on how the church should function with regard to spiritual gifts. Essentially Paul is saying that spiritual gifts—no matter how profound or impressive—mean nothing without love, as if to suggest that everything we do is incomplete without love. Therefore, whenever we love in the power of the Holy Spirit, who lives in those who believe—we are shalom, or complete. As Paul continues his treatise on love, he says as much:

Prophecy and speaking in unknown languages and special knowledge will become useless. But love will last forever! Now our knowledge is partial and incomplete, and even the gift of prophecy reveals only part of the whole picture! But when full understanding comes, these partial things will become useless. When I was a child, I spoke and thought and reasoned as a child. But when I grew up, I put away childish things. Now we see things imperfectly as in a cloudy mirror, but then we will see everything with perfect clarity. All that I know now is partial and incomplete, but then I will know everything completely, just as God now knows me completely. Three things will last forever—faith, hope, and love—and the greatest of these is love. (1 Corinthians 13:8–13)

How will we know that we're finally home? Well, the most obvious indicator is that we'll see Jesus face-to-face. But beyond that, as this "love chapter" illustrates, we'll no longer need all the other gifts of the Spirit that God gave the church so that we could *be* the church—which you'll remember, of course, is to love. But we'll still be exercising the fruit of the Spirit—which, if you recall, is love—and therein continuing to *be* his church without ever having to *go* to church. Being the church then and there will be the same thing as being the church here and now—loving God and each other, forever.

That's when we'll be finally home.

One of my favorite poets is the songwriter and performer Jon Foreman, of the band Switchfoot. He expressed being finally home very well in his song "This Is Home," written for the soundtrack for the movie *Prince Caspian* from the Chronicles of Narnia series. He says in part,

This is home,
Now I'm finally where I belong.
I've been searching for a place of my own,
Now I've found it, maybe this is home.

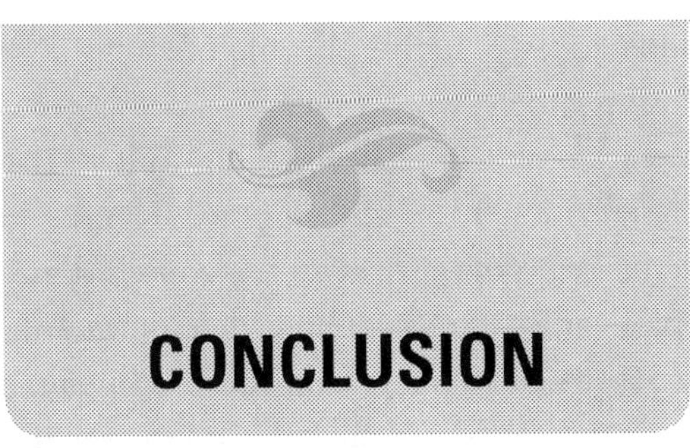

CONCLUSION

I guess when it all comes down to it, God simply wants to prepare us in this life for what he has waiting for us in the next. It never was his intention for us to *go* to church. But he has always desired for us to *be* his church. And that means that we have to be made new in him through forgiveness and resurrection.

Adam and Eve were given a shot at a life reflecting the image and character of God, and for a short while they represented what it meant to be created in the image of God. That image included not only their reflecting the character of God but also their having an intimate relationship with God. Sin, by their own choosing, slammed the door shut on both of those glorious realities. And they were forced into a life of godlessness and homelessness.

But God always had a plan in mind to help us find our way back home. Jesus would leave his heavenly home to pay the penalty for the sin that separated us from God and ushered us all into spiritual homelessness. He showed us in the way he lived his life what God had always intended our life to look like. And after dying on the cross to take our sin away, he rose from the dead as a guarantee that this God-pleasing life that he demonstrated could be ours again.

And then, as he prepared to leave this earth and return to his Father in heaven, he clearly called for his disciples to continue what he started and remain faithful to making disciples and loving others until he returned. He sent the Holy Spirit to empower them (and us) with this new and transformed life of love. While on earth Jesus lived *with* his disciples, having sent his Spirit he now lives *in* us. We are now the living, visible presence of Christ in the world. We are his hands and feet of tangible love until he returns. When people see us and experience our love for them, they experience Jesus. Living this life of loving others and making disciples who do the same is what it means to truly *be* the church.

For several years now I have been trying to help the people of Tri-County Church transition from the traditional understanding of *going* to church to the biblical notion of *being* the church. I'm so proud of the many who are embracing this incarnational paradigm. Among our church family, this philosophy of ministry and mission is gaining traction. As Christ followers move from our culture's consumer mindset of being served as it relates to going to church, to becoming contributors who exemplify the selfless servant's heart of Jesus by being the church, we truly will be a part of bringing about God's kingdom on earth as it is in heaven.

It is my prayer that you, as a seeker or a follower of Christ, will do the same, and that the local church family you are a part of can collectively embrace this idea as well. I hope you will agree with me that we should never simply *go* to church again. And then you can say along with me, "I don't *go* to church. I *am* the church."

ABOUT THE AUTHOR

Dave Bish is a husband, father of four, pastor, teacher, and church planter. In the summer of 1995 Dave moved his family to a small town in central Pennsylvania to, as he likes to say, "Do church differently." That's when Tri-County Church was born, and that's where, for the last eighteen years, the family and staff of Tri-County Church have been living out the desire to follow Jesus and fulfill the mission of his kingdom here on earth.

Dave also has a bachelor of science degree in Education. He taught public middle school for four years and then earned a master of divinity degree in 1990 from Trinity Evangelical Divinity School. He was a youth pastor for five years in the church he grew up in and has served as the lead and founding pastor of Tri-County Church in DuBois, Pennsylvania, since 1995.

It is from this context and his other life experiences that Dave shares the vision and strategy found in this book. His hope is that whether you're particularly religions or not, you will find the idea of not *going* to church anymore, but instead *being* the church, refreshing and inspiring.